THINGS SEEN IN CEYLON

ELEPHANT & MAHOUT

After his bath this elephant is taking a little refreshment. He is nibbling the tender shoots of the nearest clumps of bamboos.

THINGS SEEN IN
CEYLON

THE DESCRIPTION OF A BEAUTIFUL ISLAND AND THE NOVEL AND INTERESTING TOWN & COUNTRY LIFE OF ITS PEOPLE

CLARE RETTIE

WITH MANY ILLUSTRATIONS & MAP

GYAN

Published by

GYAN

Gyan Publishing House
5, Ansari Road
Daryaganj, New Delhi-110002
Phone: 011-47034999, 9811692060
E-mail: books@gyanbooks.com

Distribution Network
gyanbooks.com
India, USA, Canada, UK, Australia, France

ISBN : 978-81-212-4095-6 (PB)
First Published, London, 1929

2nd Impression 2020

Printed at: Gyan Press, Delhi.

Things Seen in Ceylon
Author: Clare Rettie

THINGS SEEN IN
CEYLON

THE DESCRIPTION OF A BEAUTIFUL ISLAND AND THE NOVEL AND INTERESTING TOWN & COUNTRY LIFE OF ITS PEOPLE

BY

CLARE RETTIE

WITH MANY ILLUSTRATIONS & MAP

London
Seeley, Service & Co. Limited
196 Shaftesbury Avenue

Note for Readers who Intend to Visit Ceylon

JANUARY and February are usually considered the best months in which to visit Ceylon, though March is sometimes equally good. At that time of year, the heavy rains of the north-east monsoon having ceased, the climate is cool and pleasant; shooting in the low country is better than at other times, and travelling in the wilder parts of the Island is comparatively easy, as the roads are then in good condition.

It is not desirable to travel in Ceylon during the months of October, November, and December on account of the torrential rains and consequent flooding of the roads, which makes motoring, in some parts, impossible.

April, May, and June are considered by residents to be specially healthy, and there is certainly very little fever then, but to those who are not acclimatized the heat is likely to prove trying, and on that account, those months had better be avoided by visitors.

August and September will appeal to travellers who wish to see something of the social life in such places as Colombo and Kandy. The weather is cool and dry, residents—who have been away for the hottest months—will have returned; races, dances, &c., take place, and it will then be possible to enjoy some of the generous hospitality for which the Island is noted, always provided, of course, that visitors have got the necessary introductions.

Contents

Contents

List of Illustrations

List of Illustrations

List of Illustrations

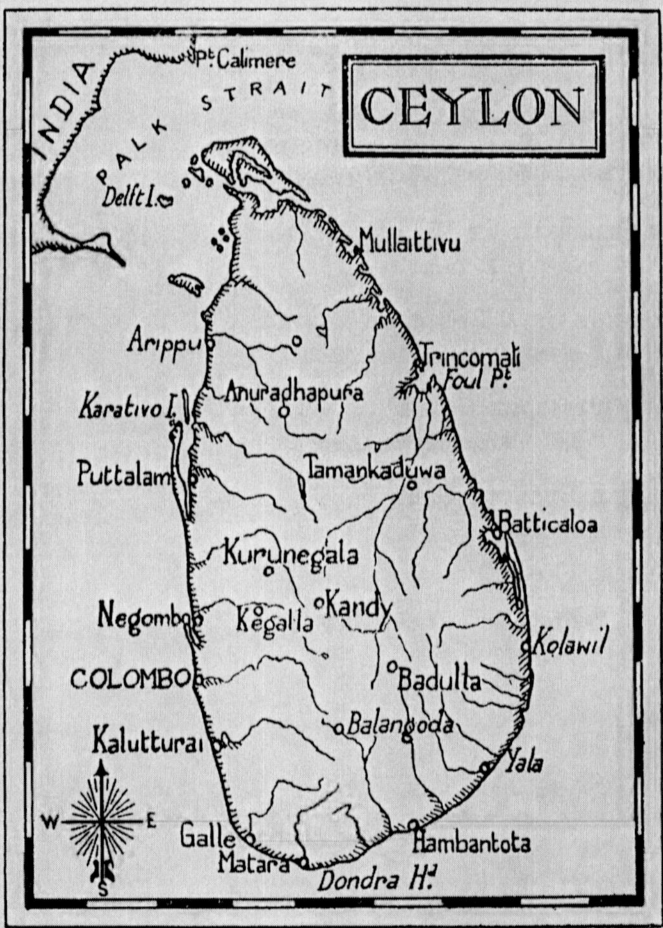

SKETCH MAP OF CEYLON

A COLOMBO TEMPLE

Though the temples in Colombo are not specially interesting the one depicted here is worth seeing. It will be found in Sea Street, & is typical of many of the Hindu Temples in Ceylon.

Things Seen in Ceylon

CHAPTER I

"THE ISLAND OF JEWELS"

THE early history of Ceylon, veiled in romantic legend, goes back some twenty-four centuries and is of great interest. Even a slight knowledge of it adds much to the pleasure of visitors, who frequently do not seem to realize that, when many of the Western nations were still in their infancy, Ceylon had a religion, art, and prosperous trade of its own.

Like Tyre, the island was "made very glorious in the midst of the Seas," and certain historians have concluded that it formed a part of the Ophir and Tarshish of the Scriptures. If that is so, it doubtless contributed some of the gold and silver, ivory and other treasures which King Solomon's ships brought back to that opulent monarch.

"The land of the hyacinth and ruby," "the new Elysium," "the jewel upon the brow of India," "Lanka the resplendent," were some of the poetical descriptions given to Ceylon in the past. Milton refers to it as "the utmost Indian isle, Taprobane," "Serendib" being another name by which it was known.

It was from India, so closely connected, historically

and geographically, with the island, that the first tradition came. It is a stirring tale of the incarnation of the god of war and wisdom, who set out to vanquish a bold, bad Titan and after fierce fighting, succeeded. He then married the beautiful daughter of a Ceylon Chieftain (to whom some of the Sinhalese priests claim to be akin) and the worthy couple—for their many virtues—are still worshipped by thousands in the East.

After a lengthy silence we get that famous epic, the "Ramayana," with its glowing description of Sita, the fair Indian queen who was kidnapped by wicked King Ravana of Ceylon. Rama, her outraged husband, is supposed to have had the passage—now known as Adam's Bridge—made for his troops to pass over, and, after terrific slaughter, to have succeeded in killing his enemy, and recovering his faithful wife. Sita, for her beauty of face and character, is still held in honour, her memory being perpetuated in Ceylon by names such as Sita-waka, Sita-ela, etc. The tale goes on that, as a punishment to Ravana for his evil deeds, part of the island was plunged into the sea. Curiously enough, scientists think Ceylon probably formed part of the Continent of Asia at one time, its geology and fauna giving reason for the supposition.

After the death of Ravana, the next interesting event of which we hear is the arrival of Wijayo, an adventurer from Northern India, and here we must note that, as the Romans claim their origin from the twins, Romulus and Remus, suckled by a wolf, so the Sinhalese—with equal pride—claim close connection with a lion. The story runs that a princess of Bengal, having fled from her home, encountered a lion, which dragged her off to a cave. There in time the unfortunate woman became the mother of a boy and girl. As the children grew up, they were—not unnaturally—terrified of their fierce father. One day their mother and they managed to escape, the furious animal pursued, but was eventually killed by his own son. This young man was known afterwards as Sinhala (the lion slayer), from which comes the name Sinhalese. He became the father of Wijayo, who founded the first dynasty in Ceylon.

The tales of Wijayo and his daring deeds are endless. It is tempting to linger over them; to tell in detail the dramatic story of the ardent Princess who, for love of him, threw herself headlong from a rock when he deserted her—but it is with the prosperity that Wijayo brought to the Island that we are chiefly concerned. He was responsible for first cultivating rice, a grain which has to be grown under water. It was for this reason that huge tanks and water courses in the Island began to be constructed.

We must pass rapidly over the long list of kings who followed, many of whom were men of culture, even of genius. The Island increased in riches, wonderful temples were built, hospitals founded for the sick, education provided for the people. Buddhism became the national religion, though other faiths were tolerated. The vast ruins that still remain in Ceylon show how great was, at one time, the knowledge possessed—how high the standard of Art and Architecture.

But there was another side to the picture. The Tamils, originally brought over from India as craftsmen to help in rice growing, began to prove troublesome—they gradually acquired power, and in time dominated the greater part of the Island, sometimes treating the Sinhalese with incredible cruelty. Then the Arabs took to visiting Ceylon, trading in elephants, jewels and spices. They settled on the coast, soon became influential politically, and by degrees got the sea ports into their own hands.

At the close of the fourteenth century, the Portuguese appeared on the scene, in an attempt to capture some of the Arab ships. They failed, but in twelve years returned and, having found favour with the Sinhalese king, were granted certain privileges. It was not long before the monarch repented his amiability and begged them to leave. They had come to stay, however, and in time took the place of the Arabs, soon making themselves detested for their religious bigotry, greed, and ambition. Some of the finest temples in Ceylon were destroyed by the Portuguese, and they were responsible for carrying off a much prized possession, the sacred tooth relic of Buddha.

The Natives struggled bravely against the hated intruders. There were desperate battles fought, and many notable victories won, but it was not until the Dutch appeared on the Island that the Portuguese were finally expelled. The new arrivals came, ostensibly to help in the war against Portugal, and their assistance was gladly accepted. Unfortunately, having achieved their end, they showed no desire to leave. They settled down, and it is to their credit that they improved the means of intercourse by canals, planted coco-nut palms, and introduced the coffee plant for the first time. They also began to cultivate cinnamon, and succeeded in getting a monopoly of that very precious commodity.

The Natives, however, who liked them at first, were soon exasperated by their exactions, and though the intruders more than once succeeded in getting into the heart of the king's possessions, they were unable to hold the interior. It was not until the eighteenth century that the British came to Ceylon. A book, which appeared not long ago, tells how their coming was due to the agency of a Scotsman, who was at one time Professor of Natural History in the University of St. Andrews. This interesting and romantic character (Hugh Cleghorn by name) was obliged to give up his Professorship because of his insatiable desire for travel and adventure. He was employed by the British Government on Secret Service, and became friends with a certain Swiss Count, proprietor and colonel of a Swiss Infantry Regiment, in the employ of the Dutch East India Company, then in Ceylon. Cleghorn was interested in the Island. He suddenly had an idea that, if he could persuade the Count to transfer his regiment from the Dutch to the English service, annexation might be possible. The Home Government, when approached, proved sympathetic, and having induced the Count to accede to his wishes, the enterprising Professor set out on his adventure. Holland had at that time fallen into the hands of the French Republic, and the Dutch Stadtholder, anxious to save the more distant colonies from the same fate, gave orders that any troops sent to the East by His British

Majesty, were to be allowed into the ports. Cleghorn's scheme was an entire success. The Natives were tired of the Dutch, who only offered a feeble resistance, and surrendered, on terms, to the British.

The East India Company at first claimed the Island, but rebellions broke out; the French (then at war with Britain) made trouble; there was constant fighting, and the British Government insisted on annexation to the Crown. It is interesting to note that Cleghorn, after receiving a substantial monetary reward for his services, returned to Ceylon as first Colonial Secretary.

The King of Kandy (then the capital of the Island) laid claim to many titles—"Emperor of Ceylon," "Prince descended from the Golden Sun," "He before whom all elephants bow," "Lord of the fishery of pearls," being only a few. He was unable to live peacefully with the British, and when, by his orders, several of them were seized and murdered, it was considered time to depose him.

The Sinhalese Chiefs had to submit, after a time, to be guided by British civilians. Good government brought peace, prosperity and contentment, a state which, in spite of occasional difficulties, happily continues to this day.

THE PETTAH

The palm-thatched bullock carts move slowly along in the less crowded parts of the Pettah & the motors which sometimes flash by always seem sadly out of place.

CHAPTER II

COLOMBO—MOUNT LAVINIA—NEGOMBO

"The use of travelling is to regulate impressions by reality, and instead of thinking how things may be, to see them as they are."

THERE are always noise, bustle, and confusion when a steamer puts into port, some slight physical difficulty in walking on a deck that no longer rises and falls, and it is certainly hot on arrival in Colombo—but none of those things can really mar the pleasure of the first view of the fascinating capital of Ceylon. For some time the majestic mountains have been seen—Adam's Peak standing out conspicuously in the centre, and it has been possible to get some idea of the pear-shaped "island of jewels;" then, as the steamer gets nearer land, the fine breakwater is passed; there comes an impression of brilliant colouring; of dark-eyed Natives in quaint canoes; and of lovely spreading trees and feathery palms, that fringe the shore.

When the launch that conveys passengers reaches the jetty, it is all a little bewildering—the shouting in strange languages, constant hooting of motor-horns and tinkling of bells, the vivid red roads and curious odours—not all of them fragrant. Rick-shaw coolies, stripped to the waist, their lithe brown bodies damp and glistening, lie in wait, and directly they have discovered which hotel is wanted, spirit passengers off, in their small-hooded carriages, through the streets, or by the side of the bluest of blue seas.

There are several good hotels, one of the best being the Grand Oriental (commonly known as the G. O. H.), and the Galle Face. The first is not far from the landing stage, with a very good view over the harbour where, at times, as many as forty to fifty big liners may be seen, their different flags fluttering in the breeze. There are huge colliers too, with dull red sides, from which coal sent down by shoots falls noisily—to be heaped in barges by half-clad men, so coal-begrimed that they look as if they had come from the nether regions; and trim sailing boats; fidgety little tugs; sometimes picturesque Maldive "buggaloes." The break-water is a wonderful sight during the Monsoon, when enormous waves dash with wild fury against its sides, throwing up great masses of feathery spray, which sparkles like silver in the sunshine—but at every season there is much of interest to be seen, both in and about Colombo harbour.

Near the principal entrance to the Grand Oriental Hotel, a number of Natives are always loitering—guides of sorts; touts for the cheaper hotels; snake charmers anxious to show what they can do with their baskets of wriggling reptiles; and vendors of odds and ends likely to appeal to the innocent Globe Trotter—who may not suspect that some of the "Indian" brass boxes, cobra candlesticks, etc., were made in Birmingham. For a time those voluble Natives, with their smiles and blandish-ments, are quite amusing, but very soon their attentions become irksome. The strong deal with them firmly, the weak buy things they do not really want, engage a hopelessly incompetent guide, or get whisked off to some unsuitable hotel.

Inside the G. O. H. a cosmopolitan crowd of passengers, from different steamers, are usually moving about—coming and going restlessly. Some are obviously excited, others a trifle dazed by their unaccustomed surroundings. A few are unsuitably clad, garments made of thick tweed, for instance, look sadly out of place. It is unwise to wear delicate shades, such as mauve or blue, because they fade very quickly in the fierce sun. White turns a sickly pale pink, as a result of the fine red dust, and is also better avoided when possible. Clothing made of some simple washing material is really the most practical, and, during the hottest part of the day, it is always advisable to wear sun *topees*. As the latter are not exactly becoming, it is consoling to know that a well-lined sunshade, or umbrella, will meet the situation.

The Galle Face Hotel is a little way out, close by the sea, in a grove of tall palms. To idle in its pleasant verandah, after a tiffin that has included appetizing Sinhalese curry, and unfamiliar but delicious fruits, is a joy. As one lingers there, a motley crowd passes: Sinhalese, the men scarcely distinguishable by their dress from the women, their hair knotted up behind and adorned with high, round combs of tortoiseshell; dusky Tamils, many with peculiar marks on their foreheads, put there in connection with some mysterious religious rite; Burghers (descendants of the Dutch), Moors, in quaint brimless hats; Afghans, Malays, Eurasians and pale-faced Europeans; all are intent on business or pleasure.

On the floor of the verandah a gentle old Sinhalese woman squats, spreading filmy lace round her, and looking wistfully for buyers. Several ingratiating Natives display glittering jewellery set with stones found in Ceylon—opalescent moonstones, star sapphires, rare cat's eyes, rubies, etc.; many are only imitation, but they flash bravely in the sunshine, as their sellers offer them, in amusingly broken English, mixed with up-to-date slang. In one corner a Native of India is telling fortunes to a group of lively Americans, in another a compatriot of his is offering, for a few rupees, to do the famous mango trick. Bronzed men from the tea and rubber estates lounge in long chairs shouting imperiously for iced drinks, which the attentive "Boys" (all waiters in Ceylon are addressed as "Boy" no matter what their age may be) hasten to bring.

The moist heat of Colombo is trying, but as the day goes on a pleasant breeze ruffles the tops of the palms, and it is possible to drive, or even walk, in comfort. It is better to dawdle in a carriage or rickshaw than to be whirled along by motor in a cloud of red dust, red because of the cabook (laterite) with which the roads are made. The drive along Galle Face is delightful—it is a very wide lawn over a mile in length, with three roads passing through it, one by the sea, another—in the centre—for commercial purposes, and the third by the side of the clear blue lake. On the lawn the public are allowed to play games, and in recent years the Natives have become quite proficient at

THE WATER CART IN CEYLON

In the early morning the water cart goes its rounds to flush the dusty roads. Although it is constantly to be seen in the hot weather, it never fails to attract attention.

hockey, cricket, and football, though one can still see small Sinhalese boys, clad in skimpy wisps of muslin, playing cricket with extraordinary bats and wickets made after some unique design of their own.

An oval shaped building on the right, as one approaches the commercial part of the town, is the Colombo (European) Club. It is a cheery meeting place, and the scene of many pleasant gatherings, more especially during the popular August Race Week. Close by there stands the Victory Column, a memorial (by Sir Edwin Lutyens) to Ceylon men who fell in the great war. It takes the form of a slim white obelisk which can be seen far out at sea. In the distance are glimpses of the tower of the Anglican, and of the dome of the Catholic Cathedrals, of the Dutch Church of Wofendhal, and the spire of the Church of All Saints. A little farther on are the Military Barracks, in an ideal situation, with a wide parade ground, facing the sea.

The business part of Colombo is known as the Fort—the name is all that remains of the fortifications that were there in the days of the Dutch. It is intersected by about half-a-dozen streets, shaded by lovely trees; Suriyas, with their fragile primrose blossoms; Spothadias; "Pride of India"; Flamboyants covered with gorgeous flame-coloured flowers; and "Rain" trees, so called because, at night, their leaves curl into a sort of tiny sack in which moisture condenses. At sunrise, when they uncurl, this moisture falls in a miniature shower.

In the most important street in the Fort (Queen Street), there is the Residence of the British Governor. It is not exactly imposing, but, veiled under graceful spreading boughs and a tangled mass of creepers, has a beauty of its own. Opposite to it is the General Post Office, of which the town is justly proud, for it is a handsome building. There are, in addition, various Government offices, the Legislative Council Chambers (new, and more elaborate ones are in course of construction), Banks, Consulates, etc. A delightful terraced garden, the gift of a former Governor (Lord Stanmore) in honour of Queen Victoria's jubilee, is near by. It makes a pleasing dash of colour, with its brilliant crotons, showy plants, and "flowers that their gay wardrobes wear."

In Chatham Street one notices a curious clock tower which serves as a lighthouse; by it is a large importing house (*Caves*) where books on Ceylon—old and new—and much useful information about the Island, may be had. The German Consulate, the Mercantile Bank, a few restaurants, and several shops, are in the same street. Not far off is the Garrison Church of St. Peter's, which was at one time used for a very different purpose—it was the banqueting hall of the Dutch Governors. There is not much of interest to be seen inside, except a few memorials.

The Chamber of Commerce, several important offices, a good hotel (the Bristol) and the Victoria Arcade, are in York Street. The Native shops, of which there are several in the Arcade, are always alluring. In them are goods of every description; quaint old Sinhalese jewelry, delicate silver work, carved ivories, hand-made lace, vases and pots of beaten copper and brass, adorned with Eastern deities; odd little boxes made of porcupine quills, rich Indian silks, etc. They are not well displayed, often being heaped ignominiously on the floor. The vendors of those articles are uncomfortably pressing, and always exorbitant in their demands, though perfectly good natured when prices are reduced nearly half—sometimes even more—by the wary buyer.

The Native quarter of Colombo is beyond the Fort, and is known as the Pettah. As one drives towards it palm-thatched carts may be seen piled high with boxes of tea, or other produce ready for shipping. Those carts move slowly, to an accompaniment of grunts, and angry admonitions addressed by the drivers to the sturdy bullocks. Hackories, odd little carriages favoured by the Sinhalese, pass, their owners seated in them in a rather perilous position, with their legs dangling. One becomes conscious of a peculiar smell, not that of "spicy breezes," but of hot, semi-naked, and not over clean humanity, mixed with the pungent odour of curry stuffs of various kinds, of luscious fruits, and heavily scented flowers.

The streets of the Pettah are always crowded; different nationalities jostle each other as they bargain in shrill voices. Chetties—men from Southern India—clad airily in thin white muslin, their heads shaved bare as a billiard ball, are busy selling rice, cloth, etc. Money changers are doing active business; barbers shaving their customers in full view of everybody; cross-legged Natives play, with dirty cards, a game in which they seem absorbed; others sit cross-legged, motionless as idols, and apparently lost in contemplation—while a few consult the Astrologers, who are busy over their horoscopes. The brown babies are adorable; clad lightly in a string of beads, they toddle about, getting in everyone's way, and are comically solemn, till a few coppers make them show their pretty white teeth, in a winning smile.

The boutiques—or small shops—are piled high with vivid coloured cloths, all sorts of ingredients for curry making, betel for chewing, etc. Some have gaudy beads and cheap gew-gaws, or brass and pottery of sorts—others have strange fruits, mangos and mangosteens, papaws, passion fruit, sour sops—an endless variety. There is no privacy whatever; everything is done, frankly, in the open air. The Sinhalese and Tamil women have a fine carriage, they carry their heads, on which artistically shaped chatties (or pots) are often poised, in truly regal fashion. Their arm and ankle ornaments tinkle musically as they move, their ears and noses sparkle with coloured jewelry, and their bright cloths (or *sarongs*) are swathed round them, with a certain careless grace. Unfortunately, of late years, many Natives have adopted European, or semi-European, dress, and the result is usually disastrous. As a rule wearers at once look commonplace, sometimes purely comic. A dissipated top-hat perched uneasily on an oily black head, an old school blazer, plus fours, and bare feet (a combination actually seen), though impressive, can scarcely be considered dignified! The noise and constant movement tire one quickly, and it is a relief to leave the busy Pettah for the drive back to the Hotel, where, after dinner, it is amusing to watch gay Europeans dancing, regardless of the heat, to the latest thing in jazz bands.

The Museum

A delightful drive is that through Slave Island (so called because the Dutch kept their State slaves there), and along the flowery banks of the cool lake to the Cinnamon Gardens, where many Europeans, and some of the more affluent Natives, have their homes. There is no cinnamon now—or practically none—for it has died out, but every other tropical tree, plant, or flower, grows there in wild profusion. The pretty bungalows and larger residences are almost lost under the great banyan trees, clumps of graceful bamboos, palms, and shrubs starred with brilliant blossoms.

In the Victoria Park (which forms part of the Cinnamon Gardens), one is positively dazzled by the purple and blue creepers, scarlet, pink and lemon coloured hibiscus, crotons of varied tints, and gleaming caladiums. There is a good galloping path for riders, tennis courts, cricket field, and a golf course in the park. Quite near is the Garden Club, where a lively crowd is usually to be seen, playing tennis or croquet, idling over tea and iced drinks in the Pavilion, or standing about and—possibly !—discussing the latest scandal.

The Museum is close by ; it has interesting exhibits typical of Ceylon, and of life there in the old days. A few followers of the Prophet are generally lingering about the door of the Mohammedan Mosque not far off, its cupola and minarets glistening in the sunshine, and one notices a rather bizarre building in yellow and terra cotta—the Victoria Memorial Eye Hospital, opposite to which is the new, and most imposing, Town Hall.

" Princes " is a smart club in that neighbourhood, where outdoor games are played by energetic

Britons, after their day's work is over. Beyond are golf links, with a fine polo ground. During Race Week the scene in that part of Colombo is very gay indeed, and the racing is of a high order, people bringing their horses from long distances to take part.

It is tempting to prolong the drive for miles, but there is only a brief twilight in Ceylon, and it is unwise to stay out too late. The drive back may be by Kollupitya Road, where—on the right—there is the Church of St. Michael and All Angels. Along the route there are dark, glossy-leaved jaks, graceful tamarinds, vanilla, almond, and other lovely trees.

To the suburb of Mutwal there is a drive through a rather crowded part of Colombo, but it is always entertaining, for there are so many novel sights to attract one's attention. Sometimes pretty Parsee ladies, enveloped in filmy veils, pass in their closed carriages ; opulent Sinhalese and Tamil gentlemen, or overdressed Burghers, whirl by in flashy motors ; third class passengers, from the different steamers, wander about, chattering in various languages, and making futile attempts to escape persistent Natives who *will* attach themselves, and are so hard to dismiss. One passes the old Dutch Church of Wofendhal, which is Doric in style, and the Roman Catholic Cathedral of Santa Lucia, an impressive building, with a nave capable of holding six thousand people. The English Cathedral, not far away, cannot by any stretch of the imagination be called beautiful, though it has a fine view. In its grounds there is a College (St. Thomas') for boys, which is run on the lines of an English Public School.

THE NATIVE BAZAAR

The native bazaar (or *boutique*) is always well in evidence in Ceylon. It is a favourite meeting-place & usually a hotbed of gossip & scandal.

To the Suburb of Mutwal

The most attractive part of the drive is farther out, when a small fishing village comes into view. The fishermen's huts are surrounded by palms, plantains, orange and lime trees. Sinhalese children play on the shores of the azure sea, some of them fishing with improvised rods and hooks, but somehow managing to catch an occasional fish. The women may be pounding paddy, singing softly over their work, or weaving baskets as they gossip under the palms. The men move noiselessly on their bare feet, spreading their nets to dry in the sun, and preparing their canoes for the next fishing.

After some days in fascinating Colombo it feels good (as our American friends say) to motor out to the quiet of Mount Lavinia. That is only a few miles away, and has a delightful hotel (noted for extremely good fish tiffins and dinners), standing on a rocky headland, with a fine view along the coast. It is very restful there, to sit in the moonlight under the coco-nut and areca palms, and listen to the swish of the sea below. One turns away from it with a sigh, but the drive back is consoling—the weird noises of a tropical night, the dancing fireflies, the soft balmy air, and the intimate domestic scenes in the native huts as the car passes, are all entrancing.

To Negombo, a popular little place along the coast, one can go by car, but if time permits, it is pleasanter to make the trip by motor launch, starting from Victoria Bridge and going along the Kelani River, until a sandy bar is crossed, and a canal entered. From that point onward the scenery is perfectly enchanting. On either side are palm groves, with little huts nestling under their shade on the green banks. In the limpid water "padda" boats with brown sails, and outrigger canoes, move slowly, and one sees Natives bathing, their brown bodies half hidden by the tall reeds and white water-lilies.

There are endless pretty little creeks and back-waters which one longs to explore, but

> "Brief day and bright day,
> And sunset red,
> Early in the evening
> The stars are overhead,"

and it is necessary to go on, otherwise the return to Colombo will be a late one.

The coast of Negombo is partly sea, and partly a rather shallow lagoon. In the village there is nothing of special interest, but it is delightful to linger on the golden sands, and watch the simple fisher folk. Some of them are out on the lagoon in their primitive *catamarans*, or, if the sea is rough, they may be seen in boat-shaped rafts (made from one or two coco-nut planks) which ride in to shore swiftly on the crest of the waves. In that blissfully quiet spot, under a cloudless sky, life's troubles and worries are for the moment forgotten, and one begins to realize something of the glamour of the East.

On returning to Colombo, after those pleasing excursions, it is well to see, before turning into bed, that mosquito nets are intact, in case some wicked *poochie* (all creepy, crawly things are called "poochies" in Ceylon) gets inside. And, in the morning, while admiring the rosy lights on the sea, and the gently waving palms, it is necessary to

NATIVE PADDA BOAT

A padda boat making its leisurely way along one of the many peaceful canals.

beware lest some tame, and exceedingly impertinent, crow flies in by the open window, to dash off, in triumph, with the morning toast. Those things happen—perhaps they do to remind us, that, in spite of the beauty all around, we have not yet reached Heaven !

CHAPTER III

KANDY

"Does perfect beauty stand in need of praise at all?"

KANDY—that romantic stronghold—once the scene of treachery and bloodshed, is now a peaceful little town in a charming setting of mountain, lake, and rich vegetation. It is sometimes hot and glaring during the day, but the mornings and evenings are delightfully cool. The Queen's (there are other good hotels) is a pleasant place at which to stay, while exploring the town and surrounding country.

The journey by rail from Colombo is fascinating. At first the train passes through low country, with native villages dotted about; or by groups of thatched huts, the owners of which are busy on the terraces of the vivid green paddy—or rice—fields. One or two Sinhalese may be seen, in terrifying positions, hanging by bare brown legs, on the tall Palmyra palms, from which they extract sap to boil down, and crystallize into a coarse sugar. Others are gathering areca nuts, to mix with lime made from calcined shells, and betel leaf; this mixture they chew, an unpleasant habit which accounts for the ugly red stains on the lips of nearly every native. Some of the men may be cutting huge leaves from Talipot palms, to thatch their huts, or to use for other purposes to which that most

THE TEMPLE OF THE TOOTH

Buddhists from every part of the world visit the greatly revered temple at Kandy. It contains what many of them still believe to be a tooth of Buddha.

profitable palm can be put; while their women gather oranges, limes, and fresh coco-nuts, to sell to thirsty passengers. There are glimpses of tea and rubber estates; of cardamons and coffee bushes; of great clumps of snowy Datura lilies, amber-coloured lantana, and trails of lovely "gloriosa superba."

As the train mounts, higher and higher, the scene changes. Mighty crags begin to frown above, sheer precipices can be seen below, the line zigzags sharply, and the wild beauty of the landscape increases. Away in the distance the high mountains are veiled in a soft purple mist, dark patches of jungle on their sides. Waterfalls dash, foaming, into the depths below, and the route skirts so perilously near the edge of an abyss, that the nervous passenger is apprehensive, until the top of the pass is reached, and there is a less sensational run into Kandy.

By the shady banks of a lake which lies in a hollow, sheltered by low, forest-clad hills—European bungalows, Native houses, and places of business are scattered; in the distance the river—the Mahaweli-ganga—flows tumultuously over rocks, and the Matale and other hills stand out, sharply silhouetted against the cloudless sky.

Though Kandy, for a time the capital of Ceylon, has always been so closely connected with Buddhism, there are not many temples of interest in it, with the exception of the far famed *Dalada Maligawa*, where the tooth relic, so honoured by all good Buddhists, is jealously guarded. The temple is not beautiful, but its architecture has a certain interest, being of an ancient native type. An octagonal tower, near the entrance, was added by the last king of

Kandy, who used to watch the Perahera pageant from its balcony. It is surrounded by an ornate wall, and a moat.

Inside the Temple the air is heavy with the sickly perfume of Champac flowers, jasmine, tube roses, and other scented blossoms, brought as offerings by the devout. Yellow-robed priests move about softly, their austere faces hidden by the fans they carry; worshippers glide in and out; irreverent tourists chatter, oblivious of any annoyance they may cause. Near the entrance there are images of Buddha, in the three conventional attitudes, and many fantastic carvings and frescoes, mostly showing the awful doom awaiting evil-doers in the next world.

By a door elaborately inlaid with silver and ivory, the Holy of Holies is reached. The sacred tooth (supposed to be one of Buddha's) is kept there, that strange relic of which so many thrilling tales have been told. It is not genuine, it could not be, for besides the fact that the Portuguese carried off the original (a spurious one was afterwards palmed off on the credulous people) no human being, not even a Buddha! ever had such a tooth. It is really a bit of discoloured ivory, two inches in length and more than one in diameter—but it continues to be an object of reverence to millions. Only on rare occasions can the relic itself be seen; the *dagoba*, however, a bell-shaped shrine, standing on a silver table, is visible through metal bars. There are six smaller shrines inside it, of pure gold and sparkling with jewels. In the most gorgeous of all the tooth rests, supported on a golden lotus flower.

A very interesting part of the Temple is the

Library. It contains a large collection of ancient manuscripts on religious, historical, and other subjects. They are in Pâli or Sanskrit, written—or rather pricked—by a stylus, on strips of palm leaf. The strips are strung loosely together between elaborately decorated covers, several of which are thickly studded with gems. It is stifling in the Temple, the heat and constant movement are tiring, and it is a relief to get out into the purer air.

Kandy was so often burnt and destroyed, in its troubled past, that few of the old buildings are left. There is, however, a part of the Palace remaining and the Audience Hall, with its tall, richly carved columns of teak, and rather florid decorations, is really interesting. It is still in use, for the British Government, probably wishing that it should continue to stand for order and authority in the eyes of the Sinhalese, cleverly turned it into the Supreme Court of Justice.

In modern Kandy there are several European shops, banks, etc., also a Museum, full of specimens of Kandyan Arts and Crafts. Those buildings are necessary, of course, but look just a little out of keeping in such romantic surroundings. The Native shops are much like those of Colombo, except that some of them contain fine silver work, peculiar to Kandy, and it is still sometimes possible to pick up in them antique pieces of Sinhalese jewellery, of unusual design—at a price!

In a charming house (the Pavilion) the Governor lives, when in Kandy; it stands, white and cool, in shady gardens where it is a joy to linger. There one sees gay green lizards, or tiny geckoes, darting through the wealth of shrubs and flowers.

Occasionally a harmless snake may slither across the path, bright dragon flies and gaudy butterflies flutter everywhere; birds warble joyously on the branches; and the insects on the plants contrive to look so like the leaves and twigs on which they settle, that it comes as a surprise when they are seen to shift their position.

The sunsets are glorious. At times the distant hills are bathed in amber and gold, or tinted a rosy pink, and to wander round the lake on a moonlight night is to stray into fairyland. The stars, always so brilliant in the tropics, shine above the great spreading trees that throw dark, alluring shadows on the paths; fireflies glitter amongst the branches, and the graceful bamboos whisper softly as they sway in the scented air.

In the cool of the early morning, it is very pleasant to stroll along, above the level of the lake, by Lady Horton's walk (so called after the wife of a former Governor), from which wooded path there is a wide view of the fertile valley of Dumbara, and lovely smiling country, away to the imposing mountains beyond. Lady Ridgeway's walk is also one that should not be missed—but, indeed, all the paths that lead round, or about, the lake are most engaging.

When walking in Kandy it is always amusing to watch the people. The Ratamahatmayas (Chiefs) are very smart gentlemen indeed. They may sometimes be seen, swaggering along with their heads held high, dressed in many yards of silk or muslin, which is wound round their ample waists and tapers at the ankles, giving them a curious top-like appearance. Jackets of heavy silk brocade, with enormous puffed sleeves, are worn over shirts fastened by jewelled buttons, and confined by velvet belts embroidered in gold. The costume is completed by oddly shaped hats, also stiff with embroidery, and sparkling with precious stones. Buddhist priests pass, their yellow robes held round them disdainfully, as if to avoid the common touch. Dhobies (washermen) beat clothes mercilessly, on large stones in the lake—a drastic method of washing that is general in Ceylon. Sinhalese men swing by, with baskets of fruit or vegetables balanced on *pingos* (yokes made of fibrous, supple wood, on which burdens of equal weight are suspended at each end)—or sellers offer *gram*, a sort of small pea, which is eagerly bought by Natives as a mild refreshment.

If visitors are in Kandy during August they will see that weird, barbaric pageant known as the Perahera. It is held in commemoration of the victory of the Sinhalese over the Tamils, in the second century B.C. Originally for the glorification of four Hindu deities, it has now become almost entirely Buddhist in character. The sacred tooth relic, in its golden shrine, takes the most prominent place in a procession, which, for several days, makes a round of all the Temples in the neighbourhood. The night before the pageant ends is perhaps the most interesting from the visitor's point of view. It is a strange cavalcade which then wends its way through the streets, under the flare of thousands of flickering torches. Elephants, kept by the Ratamahatmayas of the district, and brought in from the estates for the occasion, play an important part. They are almost completely covered with gorgeous trappings, one animal—the largest—being nearly lost under its richly embroidered and bejewelled accoutrements, even its tusks being enclosed in dazzling sheaths. On this elephant is placed, with great ceremony, a howdah containing the sacred tooth relic in its golden shrine. Two smaller elephants accompany it on either side, while Native Headmen, in festive garments, mount the others. They are attended by retainers of sorts, who carry fantastic umbrellas that glitter with gold and silver, or baskets full of bright coloured flowers. Flags flutter everywhere, devil dancers prance before and behind, wearing hideous masks, and twisting their lean brown bodies into weird contortions; there is constant chattering in shrill voices, the crash of cymbals, blowing of pipes, and banging of tom-toms—an unholy din!

The following day at the first glimmer of dawn, a strange ceremony takes place: it is known as the Water Cutting. Under the vivid green trees, their branches bowed with sweet-scented blossoms that sparkle with dew, the procession moves towards the verdant banks of the river, where a gaily bedecked boat is waiting. Four of the Chief Priests, followed by one or two assistants, walk in dignified silence, under a canopy, and by a path covered with a strip of cloth, to the water side, and get into the boat. They are punted along for a short distance, then when it is considered that the auspicious moment has arrived a signal is given, and each priest leans over to cut, with a silver sword, a circle in the water. As he does so, one of his helpers carefully dips a bowl into the centre of the circle, and fills it to the brim. At the same moment another empties that which was filled the previous year. What special virtue water obtained in this particular way is supposed to possess it is difficult to say, but it is sacred in the eyes of the Native, who no doubt attaches to it some mystic meaning. The boat having returned to the shore, the priests rejoin the procession, which—after certain rites have been gone through, returns to the Temple of the Tooth, and the Perahera is over. Though the Sinhalese have not quite the same enthusiasm for this pageant as they had in days gone by, and much of its former grandeur no longer exists, it still remains a unique and characteristic spectacle.

The Royal Botanical Gardens of Peredeniya, only a few miles out from Kandy, are noted for their beauty all over the world. It seems hopeless to try and describe them, for it would take far too long to tell of the rare trees and plants, the avenues of stately palms, the unusual fruits and flowers. There are strange parasites of every description, and cacti which grow, in some cases, to a height of nearly forty feet, their exquisite white blooms only opening their petals in the moonlight. The noble Talipot palms, with enormous leaves, have a special interest when showing their creamy wax-like blossoms—they only do so once in fifty years, then, having made their supreme effort, they fade away and die.

What a wealth of colour there is! Even on the paths there is frequently a thick powdering of mauve, pink, or orange—it comes from the fallen petals of the flowers. Homely things are growing, tapioca, arrowroot, cloves, nutmegs, ginger, etc., in the same garden with lofty palms, and trees to which are attached magnificent orchids, or festoons of flowering creepers. Peredeniya is a veritable Paradise for those interested in botany, chemistry, or entomology. There are specialists in those, and kindred subjects, attached to the gardens. They are always willing to give help, or advice, to those who may be interested..

But for the ordinary visitor it is enough just to wander under the graceful spreading boughs,· to listen to the birds, and absorb the loveliness of it all. In case it may be imagined that perfection has been reached in that enchanting spot, it is perhaps well to mention that there *are* such things as snakes to be seen (and most carefully avoided!), sometimes after rain, when they like to bask in the sun. Cobras are by no means unknown in Ceylon, and the deadly Tic-polonga is also to be found; but less harmful snakes are more common, and there is no real danger if one is reasonably careful. Bloodthirsty little leeches lurk in the grass if it is wet, and the timid may feel anxious if they happen to notice sinister looking objects hanging head downwards from some of the trees. They are flying foxes, which keep that peculiar position during the day, but when night comes spread their clumsy wings and fly about, helping themselves liberally to the ripe fruits, and making considerable noise in the process. Those queer bird-like animals (really a kind of large bat), are harmless if left alone, but are said to fight fiercely with their formidable claws and sharp teeth if attacked. After all is said and done, however, the drawbacks to a visit to Peredeniya are few—they are very soon forgotten, in the magic of those matchless gardens.

ALUWIHARA ROCK TEMPLE

The rock temple in which the teachings of Buddha were first written down —90 B.C. A place greatly venerated by all devout Buddhists.

CHAPTER IV

ROCK TEMPLES AND ANCIENT CITIES

"The world's a bubble and the life of man, less than a span."

IT is, of course, impossible to describe the wonders of the ancient cities of Ceylon in one short chapter, for a detailed account of their extensive ruins would fill a volume. One can only hope to convey some slight impression of their extent and former grandeur. The best way to reach them, if time admits, is to motor from Kandy, stopping at will to visit three very interesting places, not far off the route—Alu-Wihara, Dambulla, and Sigiri. There are several Rest Houses (bungalows provided by Government for the use of travellers) at which to stay when necessary. They are usually clean, though by no means luxurious, and the vagaries of the native Rest House keeper frequently prove amusing.

Alu-Wihara is near Matale, a pretty little town enclosed by mountains, where some of the most important Kandyan Chiefs have always had their residences. The Natives there are noted for the excellence of their carving on ivory, and for the chasing of the elaborate swords carried by Sinhalese on ceremonial occasions. A long shady street, full of rather attractive shops; pleasant open spaces;

lawns of cool green; and a public garden a-bloom with fragrant blossoms, add to the charm of Matale, but its chief interest is to be found a short distance out—at Alu-Wihara. There, amongst great rocks and gnarled trees, are rough caves containing pictures and statues of Buddha. In one of them the most casual visitor must surely feel some thrill, for in it (in the first century B.C.) were written down, for the first time, the *Sutras*, or sayings, of the great Teacher. Four centuries had passed, since (according to the belief of his disciples) he had attained Nirvana. Some error might have crept into his teaching in the long interval, but to have his words of wisdom for ever in writing—what a joy to his faithful followers! No wonder they regard the little cave in which the work was carried out—by monks chosen by the Sinhalese king for their learning and piety—with something like awe. From a tiny pagoda, built on a pinnacle of one of the rocks, it is possible to look down over the titanic boulders, past the mysterious caves that are tucked in them out of sight, to the path that seems lost in an abyss far below. It is a wild, romantic spot.

Dambulla is twenty-eight miles farther on. As far as Nalanda, which is about half way, there are cocoa and rubber estates dotted about, but beyond there is very little cultivated land, only patches of jungle, thick undergrowth, and wooded plains. On a flat plateau the rock of Dambulla stands out conspicuously. It is five hundred feet high, and out of it are hollowed the most curious temples in Ceylon. A very steep, but picturesque stairway, unevenly hewn, leads to caves which are near the top. They were used in the first century B.C. as

THE FAMOUS LION ROCK—SIGIRI

The rock to which the wicked Kasyappa fled, after committing a terrible crime. There are several most interesting remains to be seen at Sigiri.

hiding places by the same Sinhalese king who had the sayings of Buddha written down. He had been dethroned by the Tamils, and when happier days came, showed his gratitude to the gods by turning the caves into temples.

The outside, under the frowning rock, is left in its natural rude state, except for the entrances, which are modern and quite hideous. Inside, the caves are dimly lit, strangely uncanny, and a rumour that cobras (regarded as sacred by the Natives) are sometimes left to wriggle there without interference, adds to the nervous feeling one has on entering. By the door, carved from the solid rock, is a figure of Buddha, over forty feet in length. The great Teacher lies prone, wise, compassionate, serene, though an alien deity, Vishnu, is actually facing him. There are other Hindu gods as well, most of them glittering with tawdry jewellery, and with pathetic little offerings laid in front of them. In all the chambers (the central one is said to be a hundred and sixty by fifty feet, and at the entrance three feet high) there are images of Buddha, objects of worhip, and one or two statues of kings—the most interesting being that of the monarch who converted the caves into temples; his statue is of wood, and represents a corpulent, rather imposing personage. The ceilings and sides of the caves are covered with fantastic pictures, several of the frescoes being over two thousand years old. Some make one smile, such as that depicting Wijayo trying hard to land in Ceylon, while perfectly gigantic fish swim round wildly, in a frantic effort to prevent him. Those eerie dark caves, tenanted only by an ascetic looking priest and a few barefooted Natives, have an uncanny effect on the visitor. But outside the sun is shining, the soft green of the paddy fields, the view over the lovely Kandyan country, make a delightful contrast, and one is glad not to have missed those strange rock temples.

The road to Sigiri winds along for some way through jungle astir with life. Monkeys swing on the branches overhead; shy brown squirrels scuttle off at the least movement; a lazy iguana or sprightly chameleon may cross the path; there may be a flash of turquoise as a kingfisher flies by, while everywhere gorgeous large butterflies, of the most brilliant and varied colour, flutter in the sun. After a time the road comes out into open country, where the fresh sweet scent of lemon grass is a delight, and then—suddenly—from the plain, comes in view the lonely crag of Sigiri.

A tragic story is connected with this isolated place. One of the princes, Kasyappa by name, having usurped his father's throne, seized and threw him into a deep dungeon, where he walled him up—alive! To escape the fury of the people he then fled with his followers to Sigiri, where they proceeded to make an impregnable fortress. Very skilfully they constructed a spiral stairway, round the almosy perpendicular rock, surrounding it with a strong rampart. The wretched Kasyappa, becoming terrified of revenge in this, or punishment in the next, world, built huge monasteries, and granted lands, with various other privileges, to the priests, in the hope of placating the gods. But in vain. A brother of his, who had been in India, returned strongly supported, and marched to avenge his father's cruel death. There was wild

AT ANURADHAPURA

The Buddha at Thuparama Dagoba. Some idea of its size may be had by noting the native squatting near. A wonderful sense of peace is given by this crude figure.

fighting, Kasyappa was defeated, and, fearful of what his fate might be, took his own life. Perhaps his evil spirit still haunts the rock, for some sinister influence seems to linger there. Nevertheless it is well to climb to the top. There is just a possibility of falling over a precipice (less likely since a kind Government has provided handrails), or being stung by the swarms of angry bees that frequently buzz round the rock, but the still bright frescoes, carved throne, strange winding galleries, and a glorious view over the shimmering water of the little lake below, on to the Kandyan hills, make it well worth while to take some risk.

After Sigiri, the vastness of the oldest of the ancient cities—Anuradhapura (names there are, like everything else, on the grand scale !)—now so silent and deserted, is most impressive. The ruins of its former splendour can be seen for many miles—great bell-shaped dagobas (or shrines), smothered in trailing creepers ; slender pillars and sculptured stones ; mutilated statues ; remains of luxurious baths, and broken vessels from the temples, are scattered everywhere. One thing seems to have defied the march of time to some extent—the sacred Bo tree (*ficus religiosa*) in the Mahamegha Gardens, surely the oldest tree in all the world. Besides its great age (it is said to have been planted two hundred and eighty-eight years B.C.), and the fact that it is reverenced by millions of Buddhists, it fascinates because it was grown from a branch of the very tree under which the august Buddha attained wisdom. It is said that the conflict for his soul, between the powers of good and evil, was so grievous that the leaves of all Bo trees tremble to this day—they do, whether that be the reason or not.

It was the Princess Sangamitta (whose saintly brother Prince Mahinda introduced Buddhism to Ceylon) who brought the branch of the sacred tree from India, and its arrival was marked by all sorts of miraculous happenings—at least according to that ancient, and very poetical, chronicle, the *Mahawansa*. The tree, alas! is gradually shrinking, only two rather sickly boughs remain, but it still seems to produce an amazing number of leaves, for no visitor to " The Victorious, Illustrious, Supreme Lord, the sacred Bo Tree " (to give it the correct title), fails to carry away at least one leaf—and it would surely be ungracious to doubt its genuineness. The outer walls which enclose the tree are obviously of great age. There are a few statues of Buddha scattered about, and some rather fine " moonstone " steps, but the old, old tree in which some life still lingers, seems to hold one's attention to the exclusion of everything else.

The Brazen Palace, a famous monastery quite near, was so called because its roof was covered with brass. It was originally an immense building supported by no fewer than sixteen hundred monolithic columns, the majority of which are still standing. They cover several acres of ground—a wilderness of pillars. Two curious monuments, the King's and Queen's Baths, are not far off, as well as the important Ruanweli, or Gold Dust Dagoba, which has been partially—and not altogether happily—restored. One notices by it a time-worn statue of one of the kings; a small model of the dagoba itself; the large court for elephants which took part in

THUPARAMA DAGOBA

One of the most famous dagobas in the ancient city of Anuradhapura. Though restored it keeps its ancient character & is very impressive.

processions; and a few other remains that are of interest, but Ruanweli, with its dreary expanse of brick, its rather shapeless summit overgrown with shrubs and stunted trees, is difficult to picture as it was in its palmy days.

It is a delightful road that leads on to the next Dagoba (that of Thuparama), past wide lawns shaded by beautiful trees; here and there through the branches can be seen massive granite columns, broken statues, and "moonstone" steps with their graceful designs of the lotus flower, sacred geese, elephants, and other animals. One group of pillars, near by, is generally known as "The Queen's Pavilion," though it may have been part of a monastery.

The Thuparama Dagoba dates back to 307 B.C. and is the oldest of all the ruins in Ceylon. It has been restored several times, but seems to have kept much of its original character, the rings of tall, elegant pillars, which surround it, being of special interest. Tradition has it that the right collar-bone of Buddha is enshrined under the massive brick work, and that, when being carried by elephants to its resting place, the relic behaved in a decidedly erratic fashion, for it suddenly rose, hurled itself into the air, and, surrounded by lurid flames, showed itself to an astonished multitude! Beyond this Dagoba one sees the Basawak Kulama Lake which is supposed to have been made, for irrigation purposes, well over two thousand years ago. There are three lakes in the neighbourhood of Anuradhapura, each with its own peculiar charm.

If Thuparama is the oldest, Abhayagiri Dagoba is certainly the largest in the Island. Its height is said to have been four hundred and fifty feet, and it still covers eight acres of ground, with a mass of ruins. Jetawana-rama, which is in an equally ruinous condition, is also immense. The Ratna Pasade (or Jewel Palace) has one exquisitely carved slab or "guardstone" worth seeing, and the once gorgeous "Peacock Palace" has some rather fine pillars and carvings on stone, which are all that remain of its former magnificence.

In a romantic setting, near lovely woodlands and large pools of cool water on which float pink and white lotus lilies, there is a fascinating little temple called Isurumuniya. It was discovered some years ago, concealed in dense jungle, and was, happily, restored. The doorway is quite beautifully carved, inside are whimsical frescoes and sculptures in bas-relief, with the usual sphinx-like Buddhas. It is a pity that some of the restorations are far from artistic, but nothing can take from the romance of its situation, and the curious carvings, of unusually sprightly elephants, on the rock outside, are delightful. If the same gracious old Sinhalese priest, who used to be there, is still in charge, it will be found a real pleasure to linger and listen to his philosophy of life, told in quaint, child-like English. His curiously expressed, but obviously sincere, blessing, will not soon be forgotten.

Eight miles out from the old City is the Hill of Mahintale. It is specially interesting as having been the meeting place of Mahinda and King Tissa, who was his first convert to Buddhism. There is a very fine stairway, with over a thousand large granite steps, which leads to Ambustela Dagoba, near the summit, in which the ashes of Mahinda were laid.

It was erected on the spot where the king and the saint were supposed to have met—Tissa having been enticed there by a goddess disguised as a deer, or so the *Mahawansa* gravely informs us. There are endless monuments scattered about on the hill; one that is always admired is the Naga Pokuna, or snake bathing pool. By the side of it, carved on the rock, is a huge cobra in bold relief.

On a narrow, exceedingly precipitous ledge overlooking a superb view, is a rough couch hewn from the rock, which is said to have been Mahinda's bed. Poor Prince Mahinda! All his philosophy and love of contemplation must have been needed to console him for the discomfort of that hard couch. The ancient Dagoba, at the very summit of the mountain, is the Etwihara. In it one precious hair from the head of Buddha is supposed to be enshrined—the size of the building seems a trifle out of proportion to that of the relic! No one, however, will grudge the climb, for the view from the top is simply glorious. There were monasteries and other buildings on the hill, and amongst the ruins one can still see inscriptions which are perfectly legible. They tell of the life and discipline of the monks who once lived there.

The comparatively few Natives, who now make their homes at Anuradhapura, look somewhat sad and depressed, though, fatalists like all Orientals, they never complain. It is to be hoped that, in the future, some of its former prosperity may be restored to the old City. The comfortable modern hotel, and the many tourists who now visit Ceylon, and its famous ruined Cities, may do something towards this good end, even though, as it must be confessed, they both look rather out of the picture. The causes of the downfall of Anuradhapura were many, chiefly never-ending struggles with Tamil invaders, cruel wars that led to the abandonment of necessary irrigation works, and the consequent failure of rice crops.

Polunnuruwa, about fifty miles to the south-east, took the place of the older City as capital, and soon almost outdid it in splendour. To the noblest of the Sinhalese kings (Parakrama) and his wonderful statemanship, its prosperity was due. The vast ruins show clearly how great must have been his riches and power. On the high embankment of the lake, there is a weatherbeaten, but impressive, statue of this great Ruler. He stands, with his back to the City, holding an ola (or palm leaf) book, in which he seems absorbed. The ruins of his palace are still to be seen, with walls that are of brick, and enormously thick. In the Pavilion there are several frescoes adorned with lions and elephants, and near by is the Kumara Pokuna—or bath of the Prince—the broken pillars and other fragments of which show it must have been a very luxurious bathing place indeed. Just beyond the wall of the palace there are several temples. In one (the Dalada Maligawa) the sacred Tooth Relic was kept for a time. It is a little temple which has considerable charm. The Siva Devale 11, not far distant, is distinctly Hindu in character, as are a great many of the monuments at Polunnuruwa. One shrine, prettily named "The Flower Altar of Nissanka," is most artistic in its decoration of pillars, and has four stairways leading to a court.

A little way out one finds the Jetawana-rama

Dagoba, which has stood the passage of time better than most of the buildings, doubtless because its walls are particularly thick. The columns on either side originally propped up an arch, part of which still remains. There is a passage, then a cell occupied by an immense headless Buddha. This dagoba is almost purely Hindu in style, and is supposed to have been built by workmen brought over from India at a time when Buddhism was languishing in Ceylon. The religion revived later, but shows many traces of Hinduism to this day.

The Gal-Wihara temple should not be missed, if only for the three cleverly sculptured figures to be seen there. One represents Buddha seated; another, which is huge, shows him after his spirit has reached Nirvana; the third is that of his best loved disciple, "Ananda," who looks with unutterable sadness, yet resignation, at his dead master. All three figures are cut from a wall of granite.

Near the Rest House, which is close by the Topa-Weya Lake, King Parakrama had his Pleasure Garden, and there are also the ruins of what were the Council and Audience Halls of one of the kings. But Polunnuruwa shared the same fate as the older City; population and wealth have gone long, long ago. Its parks and gardens, once so lovely, if we may believe the *Mahawansa*, are now lost in the dense jungle, and one turns away from it, struck with "the sad vicissitude of things."

CHAPTER V

TRINCOMALEE AND JAFFNA

" Far from gay Cities and the haunts of men."

TO motor on to Trincomalee, that fine port with one of the most picturesque harbours in the world, will delight lovers of wild scenery, as much as it will satisfy those who are keen on sport. Part of the route runs close by some of the immense lakes so skilfully constructed long ago, through stretches of open plain, and by thick jungle.

When stopping overnight, at one of the many Rest Houses to be found on the way, it is a novel experience to wander in the dusk close to the jungle and learn something of its peculiar spell. Away in the distance an elephant is trumpeting, there is the prolonged howl of jackal or shrill bark of pariah dogs, boars are grunting, frogs croaking hoarsely, and sometimes that dread owl—known as the devil bird—is moaning like a lost soul in torment. There are reptiles about; they may not be visible, but the rustling in the undergrowth shows that they are not far off. Trails of white Datura lilies look like ghosts in the dim light, and the boughs of the tall trees whisper and crackle mysteriously, as they cast dark shadows. One begins to understand why the superstitious Natives think evil spirits lurk in the dark.

A Rest House

At the Rest House, later, an obsequious Sinhalese leads the way, ceremoniously, to the room which he has hastily prepared. He carries a lighted candle (usually stuck in an empty beer bottle by way of candlestick), round which all sorts of tiny insects circle madly. There are several dark objects hanging from the ceiling, which look suspicious. "That nothing," he remarks casually, in answer to an anxious inquiry, "that only bats"—and leaves his visitor to get into bed, and as likely as not to listen to rats and rat-snakes holding high jinks overhead. Fortunately there is a thick ceiling cloth, which effectually prevents their falling through; in any case motoring in the sweet scented air has a soporific effect; rats, bats, and snakes are soon forgotten in slumber.

After motoring through country where Wanderoo monkeys frolic on the branches, and gibber their disapproval of all motor-cars that invade their privacy, there is a silvery gleam of water, and a lovely lake, that of Kanthalai, comes into view. Over its limpid waters, rosy with the pink of lotus flowers, hover birds with feathers that shine like jewels in the sunshine. Pink flamingoes, water pheasants, pelican, teal and duck, are among the many attractive birds that are to be seen. There are, however, other frequenters of the lake which are less pleasing, such as the clumsy mud-bespattered buffaloes, and the sinister looking crocodiles. Under the shady trees on the banks, peacocks spread their brilliant tails, tall cranes stalk about solemnly, and butterflies, large and lustrous, flutter everywhere. The great stone embankment, sluices, and canals of this lake (only one of many hundreds in

Ceylon) give some idea of the vastness of the ancient irrigation schemes, and are most impressive. It is difficult to leave a spot of such enchantment, but the rest of the way is varied, and full of interest.

The harbour of Trincomalee (or " Trinco " as it is more familiarly called) is really very beautiful. It is not symmetrical, and has two most picturesque headlands which protect it effectually against the monsoons. Verdant little islands are dotted about in its peaceful waters, the heights on its shores are warmly wrapt in vegetation, and in the distance are the majestic mountains. Trinco is well fortified, and is still of some importance as a Naval Station, but has not grown as a commercial port for several reasons, the chief being that it was never practicable to send cinnamon—once such a valuable export—from there, and later, because Colombo was a more convenient place for shipping coming through the Suez Canal.

In the gardens of Admiralty House (where the Admiral and his staff have delightful quarters), there is a huge Banyan tree, which gives the illusion, as all Banyans do, of being several trees instead of only one, because of a peculiar habit. The branches, when they become too heavy for the principal stem to support, send roots down to the ground, and those eventually grow nearly as large as the parent tree itself, so giving the impression of a group of trees. It is said that a thousand people could easily take refuge under the branches of the Banyan tree at Admiralty House, and it may be true, though it is doubtful if it has ever been put to the test.

Fort Frederick, with the headland known as Dutch

Point, encloses a bay, shaped like a horse-shoe. It is protected on three sides by strongly built walls, on the fourth by high precipitous cliffs. There is a fine view from it, away over the peaceful blue waters of the Inner Harbour, to the bold rocky coast and forest-clad hills. A few primitive guns—now used for such innocent purposes as anchoring the flagstaff, and various cannon balls that are lying about, remind one of the purpose for which the place was used so many years ago It was built by the Dutch in the sixteenth century.

Near the point of the promontory on which Fort Frederick was erected, there is an immense crag, "Saami Rock," which rises to a giddy height. A temple stood there, but it was destroyed by the ruthless Portuguese. Only the site is left of the once famous "Temple of a Thousand Columns," dedicated, before the days of Buddhism in Ceylon, to the worship of Siva. Natives, however, do not soon abandon a place which has sacred associations, and certain religious rites are still performed there from time to time.

Occasionally, at sunset, a group of men and women may be seen wending their way to the summit of "Saami Rock." They carry humble offerings of grain, perhaps a handful of champac or other sweet-scented flowers, some fruit, or incense. Those things they present to an officiating priest who, attended by his satellites, paces slowly to the extreme edge of the cliff, chanting a melancholy litany, and throws each offering into the void—a gift to the gods. He then lights a fire which he swings in a brazen censer three times, continuing to chant, while the worshippers raise their arms, appealingly, to the heavens. After sacred ashes have been rubbed on the foreheads of those taking part, the ceremony is over, and, talking in subdued whispers, as if awed by some mystic experience, all go slowly down the steep path that leads to the town below.

A pathetic story is connected with a pillar that stands on the highest peak of the rock. It marks the spot where a pretty Dutch maiden of gentle birth once watched a faithless lover sail away. He was a dashing young officer, attached to the barracks near where she lived, and she adored him. But alas ! for the falseness of men, though he had vowed to make her his wife, the day came when, no longer loving her, he decided to leave Trincomalee. The poor girl at first refused to believe he could be so cruel, and it was not until she actually saw the vessel, with the perfidious one on board, pass the cliff on which she was standing, that she realized he had gone. With a cry of despair she flung herself into the deep. Her name, " Francina Van Reede," and the date of the tragedy, are engraved on the pillar, but time has almost completely obliterated them.

It is said that the whole British Fleet might anchor in the calm, deep waters of the Inner Harbour at Trinco, but as a rule it is deserted, except for a few picturesque old ships unfit for service, some catamarans, and possibly one or two small coasting vessels. On the hills beyond is Fort Ostenburg, built by the Portuguese, largely from the materials they took from the Temple of the Thousand Columns. It is now dismantled, and the ruins almost lost in the tight embrace of fig and other trees. Among the remains of barracks, and various old buildings, a fairly modern stone stands out. It marks the spot where an unfortunate soldier fell, after being blown from a gun on the battery above, during the firing of a salute for the Emperor Frederick. There is something rather depressing about the old Fort, and one leaves it, without regret, to return to the sleepy old town.

At the bend of the bay, between Fort Frederick and Dutch Point, the town lies. The shops are not particularly interesting, but most of the houses are solidly built, with pleasant verandahs and tall pillars. Some of them, notably the old Rest House, contain fine pieces of antique Dutch furniture, of which the owners are extremely proud. The streets have Angsana, Gold-Mohur, Tamarind and Banyan trees planted near them, which give a grateful shade, and the drives along the sea front, by the harbour and beyond, are delightful.

At Kenya, a few miles out from Trinco, there are several hot springs which are held in some awe by the Natives, who tell many curious legends about them. But a more attractive place to most visitors is Kottiar, where Robert Knox was taken captive. He was British, and on a ship (the *Anne*) of which his father was captain, when they were caught in a severe storm and put into Kottiar. Unfortunately the King of Ceylon at that time had a penchant for European prisoners, so the Natives promptly captured the whole party. For over twenty years Robert Knox (his father died in captivity) lived as a prisoner. He was not ill-treated, and bore his exile courageously. In the end he was able to escape, and wrote his life and adventures. His book, which is written in a simple, artless style, has great charm; it will be enjoyed by everyone interested in Ceylon.

There is any amount of good shooting to be had within a comparatively short distance of Trinco, and sportsmen will come across most of the game, big and little, still to be found in the Island. Perhaps it may be as well to mention that an ordinary licence to shoot game does not include elephants or buffaloes, for which a special permission is necessary, and only "proscribed" rogue elephants may be shot.

To find oneself at Jaffna, a peninsula far north from Trincomalee, is like straying into a new world. It is well, if possible, to stop at Elephant Pass on the way, if only to have a meal at the picturesque old Rest House, which stands on the edge of a lagoon, and was originally part of a Dutch fort. As one gets near Jaffna, wild uncultivated country ends, and instead there are well-kept fields and low-lying land, all improved by husbandry. The people, too, are quite different, for there are practically no Sinhalese, the peninsula having been inhabited by Tamils for some two thousand years. They are a well educated, prosperous people, not unlike the Jews in some respects, for they are decidedly clannish, have a flair for making money, and are clever in many ways. They must not be confused with the Tamil emigrants who work on the tea, rubber, and other estates. Those come over from Southern India, and are very different in character.

It was at, and near Jaffna, that the great missionary St. Francis Xavier made so many Native

AT POLONNARUWA

The gigantic figure of a recumbent Buddha, 46 feet in length & cut from the solid rock, in the ruined city of Polonnaruwa.

converts to the Roman Catholic religion. His followers were persecuted, and on two occasions massacred, by order of the king, after which the Portuguese took measures to protect them. It was about this time that the original Tooth Relic was seized, and in spite of the tempting offer of a large sum of money for its restoration, was pounded to powder in a mortar, burnt, and the ashes dispersed.

There are not a great many traces left of the Portuguese, except an old monastery and church, both in ruins (they are a little way out of Jaffna), and a bell inscribed "Our Lady of Miracles of Jaffnaputam," which is preserved in the vestry of the Dutch church. This building is interesting, and though now abandoned as a place of worship, is still in good condition. It is built in the form of a Greek cross, and its size gives one some idea of the number of Dutch Presbyterians expected to worship there. Nearly all the furniture has been removed, but the Commander's pew, made from different local woods, is still to be seen, and in the organ gallery there is a quaint panel representing King David as an old man playing the harp, and looking at a book of psalms—written in Greek, and lying on an obviously European reading desk! Several of the granite tombstones, let into the floor, have beautiful carving, but what is most striking in this deserted church is its colossal size.

The Fort is built of coral, and has stood the passage of time admirably. Inside it are many fine buildings, including the Church and "King's House" which, though by no means impressive outside, has enormous rooms, the dining-room alone being 45 feet square. It was for some time used as a

Residence for the Governor, but is now the home of one of the Government officials. Many of the houses show signs of the Dutch occupation, being very solidly built, with handsome carving on their massive doors. There is nothing special to buy in the shops, with the exception of rather attractive pieces of jewellery. The goldsmiths of Jaffna were always noted for their delicate and artistic gold work, and they have not yet lost their skill.

Beyond the town are acres and acres of coco-nut and Palmyra palms, with, here and there, terraces of paddy. Tobacco is also grown in great quantities, and it is interesting to watch the Tamils watering the plants. The wells they use are very primitive; water is drawn by buckets attached to a log of wood fixed on a high post. It behaves rather like a see-saw, coolies walking backwards and forwards on the log, which acts as a lever.

The Palmyra palm, with its huge fan-shaped leaves, has uses that seem endless. The fruit, which grows in clusters on the stem, is used as a food by the more indigent Natives, and jaggery, which is prepared from the sap, is a prized sweetmeat. The seeds are eaten as a sort of vegetable, their shells used as fuel, and the leaves make excellent umbrellas, fans, baskets, mats, thatch for the huts, etc. At one time they also served for writing purposes, instead of paper. All sorts of sweet smelling spices are also grown, and the fruit in Jaffna is quite the best to be found in Ceylon.

Curiously enough, the Tamils in that part of the world have taken a leaf out of America's book, and gone "dry," so that no wine is to be had at the Rest House, though it can be got elsewhere. It is

THE ROCK TEMPLE AT ANURADHAPURA

A general view of the Rock Temple, showing how it has been restored. As can be seen it has lost, from an artistic point of view, more than it has gained.

often far too hot to be altogether agreeable in Jaffna. The wind can be very boisterous at times, too, and though it is then cooler, the fine dust which whirls along in clouds is distinctly trying. The different character of the people living there, from that of the Natives in other parts of the Island, the Portuguese and Dutch remains still to be seen, are what make it worth while to pay a visit to this rather out of the way part of Ceylon.

CHAPTER VI

NUWARA ELIYA. TEA AND RUBBER

"Thank God for tea! What would the world do without tea? How did it exist?"

THOUGH tea estates are to be seen, scattered about in many parts of Ceylon, that invaluable plant is at its best up on the hills. A short time spent in Nuwara Eliya, and in the region near that well-known hill station, gives one a very good idea of tea cultivation, and makes a delightful change from the low country. To leave the sultry heat of Colombo in the morning, and in the evening to sit comfortably by a blazing log fire, is to enjoy a piquant contrast.

The train runs through fine country, curves in an amazing fashion after Talawakelle, and in places crosses on girders that stretch from rock to rock, over deep crevices of the mountains. As Nuwara Eliya is approached, the scenery becomes increasingly wild and grand. Twisting and twining, the route goes along the side of a deep chasm, fringed with trees, the gnarled trunks of which are almost hidden under coloured lichens, long trails of moss, or clinging parasites of every description. The Keena, with leaves of vivid crimson, and other trees that have buds of purple and yellow, make the woods look gay with colour. Down in the depths below the Nanuoya river splashes over rocky

THE KEENA TREE

In Nuwara Elija, & its neighbourhood, the Keena tree may be seen at its best. The bright red leaves in the distance look like flowers.

boulders, its silvery waters sparkling in the sunshine; then, after running through a peaceful glen, with glimpses of waterfalls throwing up masses of snowy spray, Nuwara Eliya, at an altitude of 6200 feet, is reached. It lies in the middle of a grassy plain, well sheltered by towering mountains.

The air is delicious, clear and keen—just for a short time it makes one a trifle breathless, owing to the altitude. But it is very pleasant to look out of the windows of one of the many nice hotels, and see homely English flowers, such as pansies and geraniums, growing hardily. If it happens to be early morning a gnome-like coolie, wrapped in a sack which he has pulled over his head to protect him from the cold, may be picking strawberries for "Lady's" or "Master's" breakfast, and the ground may be sparkling with hoar frost.

There is always something to do in the hill station, and the walks and drives are endless. Those who are energetic will enjoy the six mile promenade round the lake, the shorter stroll to Naseby Hill, or the rather arduous climb to the top of the highest mountain in Ceylon, which rejoices in the name of Pidurutallagalla ("Pedro" for short), and is 8300 feet above sea-level. The view from the summit is magnificent, extending over hills and valleys, mountain streams and torrents; rolling downs and grassy plains—away to the sea beyond. A delightful drive—it is too far to walk—is to the wild, grand pass of Rambodde, on the way to which a fine golf course is passed; the Governor's Residence, and charming bungalows, with "red-hot pokers," flaming poinsettias, and other showy flowers in their gardens.

Games

All outdoor games are to be had in Nuwara Eliya: golf, tennis, croquet, football, cricket etc., except in June and July, when the monsoon, with its torrential rain and terrific thunder-storms, makes it necessary to stop outdoor amusements for a time. October, too, is usually wet, but even on the worst days there is generally a brief respite, when it is possible to go out for exercise. On the Race Course gymkhanas are held now and again, the chief event being the annual Race Meeting, to which Europeans come from all over the Island. Natives are also well in evidence, they thoroughly enjoy the excitement, and as they stand about, or squat in groups under the trees, their gay garments and festive turbans add a gracious note of colour.

At the United Club, for both sexes as its name implies, there is a golf course, tennis courts, a library, card-room, etc., and lively dances take place from time to time. The Hill Club, which is for men exclusively, is a favourite meeting place for sportsmen and others. Fishermen (with luck!) will find trout and carp in the river; those keen on shooting will, at the season when the lovely Nelu flower is in blossom, get plenty of jungle fowl; there is really no excuse for anybody feeling bored in Nuwara Eliya. One small drawback may be mentioned (it only exists for those anxious to keep slim!): the keen air produces a rather startling appetite. But it also whips colour into pale cheeks, and it is pleasant to see rosy children after the pale-faced mites one meets in Colombo.

A drive to the Moon Plains, so called because moonstones are sometimes found there, is enchanting. The road goes through grassy land to a thickly

PLUCKING TEA

Tea pluckers at work. The green leaf, as they pluck it, is thrown into the baskets slung over their shoulders.

wooded gorge, and on to Barrack Plain Lake, where the wild picturesque scenery reminds one of Scotland. Always, and everywhere, Natives are to be seen, sometimes quite busy, though they are adepts at doing nothing. They like watching golf, even if a trifle astonished that any game should be taken so seriously. The brown eyed, dusky little caddies, dressed in nondescript garments, are full of importance. They follow the players round, and are proud when their own particular " Dorai " makes a good shot, but give vent to their feelings in an exasperated " Ah Yoh ! " if it happens to be a bad one.

Hakgala Gardens, a few miles out, have a unique position, for they are tucked away under a frowning rock. The road leading to them is very steep, and is cut, on one side, from the rugged cliffs. It skirts along the edge of deep ravines, and passes by foaming waterfalls. The gardens are less tropical, and have not quite the same appealing charm as those of Peredeniya, but the handsome tree ferns, wealth of roses, and unexpected streams and pools full of fragile pink and white lotus flowers, are alluring. There are giant bamboos, too, with golden stems, lovely orchids clinging to the trees, and maidenhair ferns growing in every nook they can find. Brown and grey squirrels scamper about on the branches, monkeys swing from bough to bough. One sees unpleasant worms, sometimes of a curious shade of blue, crawling along. They may be quite five feet in length, and there is nothing to be said in their favour, except that they are perfectly harmless.

Some of the finest tea estates in Ceylon are near Nuwara Eliya, and thousands of acres of that most useful of plants are to be seen, with factories and bungalows close by them. Coolies—mostly over from Southern India—with picturesque woven baskets suspended by ropes from their heads, work in groups. They are plucking the leaves, weeding, or, if it happens to be the right season for that operation, pruning. Canganies (overseers) and conductors supervise them, and are responsible to the European "Dorais" (masters) for their work. It may be of interest to hear how their days are mapped out.

About six o'clock in the morning a tom-tom, horn, or whistle (it depends which particular torture in the way of noise the planter can stand !) is sounded to call the coolies to what is known as Muster. They arrive fairly punctually, chattering in shrill voices, and gathering in some open space near a bungalow, or by the factory. A few Europeans are usually present, probably two of the young assistants, and a "Creeper." It must be explained that, for some extraordinary reason (nobody seems to know why), all pupils on tea estates are called "Creepers"; the custom is universal in Ceylon.

After the coolies have been counted, and their work arranged for the day, they are sent off in gangs to pluck, weed, or whatever may be wanted. Women make the best pluckers, their thin brown fingers move with astonishing rapidity as they pluck the leaves and toss them over their shoulders into the baskets. Only a bud and two leaves from each shoot are allowed to be taken, unless tea of a coarse quality is required. It may be as well to mention here, that it is not considered correct to talk of "picking" tea, nor is it wise to tell a planter (as

SORTING TEA

Laughing & chattering the tea pluckers settle in groups to go through the leaf they have in their baskets & discard any that may be unsuitable.

some innocent visitors do) that "there is very pretty blossom on the bushes." That is a reflection on his supervision of the estate, as blossom is supposed to be removed directly it dares to appear.

Two or three times during the day the baskets of leaf are weighed, the amount plucked by each coolie noted, and the leaf taken to the factory. About four o'clock outdoor labour is over, and coolies are credited—to be paid later—according to what work they have done, usually having a few words of encouragement if it has been good, a sharp rebuke if the contrary. They take either praise or blame with equanimity, having great faith in the justice of their British Dorais. Before wandering off to their huts, or "Coolie Lines" as they are generally called, the women collect their babies, who have been peacefully swinging on the branches of one of the trees in a strip of cloth that does duty as hammock, or—if they are old enough to toddle about—have been left in the care of some old crone. One good meal each day is provided (on estate account) for children, and there are schools where, under the eye of a Native schoolmaster, the older ones are taught a few elementary lessons. They take their education very seriously, those little brown mites, looking comically solemn as they squat on the floor, and repeat their lessons in a monotonous sing-song, or add up sums, with busy fingers, on the sand which serves them in place of slates. Coolies (almost all are Tamils) are now provided, under Government supervision, with hygienic quarters. At first they were none too grateful, but are gradually beginning to appreciate the greater comfort of their homes.

After the tea arrives at the factory it is spread, rather sparsely, on jute hessian, and left to wither, the process being helped by hot air should the weather be damp or otherwise unfavourable. The Native teamaker, who is quite an important person, decides when it is ready to be put into a machine called a tea roller, which squeezes out any tannin, or moisture. It has then to be passed through a roll breaker, which sifts the leaf, by a wire mesh, into a trolly placed underneath to receive it. After being sifted it is spread out on glass tables, in what is known as the fermenting room, covered with damp cloths, and left to ferment and become the colour required. When the teamaker is satisfied that it has acquired the right tint, it is fired—that is, put through a current of hot air by machinery, until it has become dry and brittle, and after it has been cooled, it finally appears as the tea which is sold for domestic use. Different grades are arrived at by sifting through huge sieves, which revolve at great speed. The whole process of teamaking in Ceylon is a very cleanly one; it is scarcely touched by hand after it has reached the factory. If some of the tales that are told of teamaking in China are true, it is not surprising that so many people prefer that of Ceylon, quite apart from its flavour.

Since the disastrous failure of coffee in the Island (owing to a disease which attacked the leaves); that shrub has been very little cultivated, but one occasionally sees a few bushes. They have most fragrant blossoms, of a snowy white, that grow in axils of the leaves, and, later, scarlet berries that look like miniature cherries. Cocoa is grown successfully; the trees are extremely pretty, with glossy dark green leaves, and large crimson or yellow pods which contain the brown beans from which cocoa and chocolate are made. One sees cocoa growing in different parts of the Island, but chiefly in the low country. Chincona is also cultivated for the quinine that is got from the bark, and cardamons, vanilla, pepper, camphor, sago, etc.

Rubber, as all the world knows, is now one of the most important products in Ceylon, and was responsible for many fortunes made, and lost! during the famous Rubber Boom. It grows almost anywhere, but does best at an altitude of not much over 3000 feet. At one time tea and rubber were grown together, but that has practically been given up, as it proved unsatisfactory. A walk or ride through a rubber estate is full of interest; the trees give a pleasant shade, and their cool green leaves are restful to the eyes. Natives may be seen busy making incisions—"tapping" as it is called—in the bark. They have to make them with great care, as the cut must not go too deep. The milky white latex drips into the vessels (often coco-nut shells) which are ready to receive it. After being cleared of any impurities it is treated with an acid, coagulated, and turned into rubber biscuits, blocks, etc.

It is said that over four hundred thousand acres of rubber have now been planted, and it is certain that, as time goes on, the product will be increasingly required for all sorts of purposes. Probably the more sensational days of rubber may be over, but most people seem confident that it will add to the prosperity of Ceylon for many years to come.

CHAPTER VII

IN THE PROVINCE OF UVA

" The earth was made so various, that the mind
Of desultory man, studious of change
And pleased with novelty, might be indulged."

THERE is a delightful run, either by train or motor, from Nuwara Eliya to the charming little town of Badulla, in the province of Uva. At a plateau known as Horton Plains, only a few miles off the route, good hunting, shooting, and fishing are to be had, and if the Nelu shrub happens to be in bloom, it may be seen there in all its glory. The blossoms are of various shades of blue, purple, red and yellow, and have a subtle fragrance. Crimson rhododendrons, pure white datura lilies, golden-brown lantana (the last a flower which, though pretty, is becoming rather a curse in Ceylon, as it multiplies so quickly) and several kinds of orchids, all grow on this undulating plain. The air is keen and bracing, and the Rest House, below which a stream flows, if not exactly palatial, does very well for a short stay.

On continuing the route to Badulla one comes across a sudden, and unexpected, change in the scenery. After Pattipola a tunnel is cut through the rock, and on emerging from it, there appears a wide stretch of bare rolling downs that extends for

NEAR BADULLA

One of the roads leading to the pretty little town. The Hill of the Gods (Namunukula) is seen in the distance. Note the pingo carrier with his load of bananas.

many miles, broken at long intervals by patches of trees. Beyond are range after range of hills, their summits nearly always concealed under a filmy veil of purple mist. At Haputale it is well to stop in order to see the lovely Dyaluma Falls, which are not far off—at Koslanda. The waters of those falls dash from a great height over dark cliffs, and break into sparkling spray, which blows in every direction, shrouding the trees and shrubs that grow near in a fine silvery mist.

Shortly after leaving Haputale there is a transitory view of white buildings—Diyatalawa Camp—where, for two years after the South African war, five thousand Boer prisoners were kept. It is still in use, being now a recuperating station for the East Indies Naval Command, etc. Bandarawela, a little farther on, is a small village where a few Europeans and others live, induced to go there by the cool and healthy climate. There is a good hotel, and it is an excellent spot for those wishing to have a complete rest, but there are no buildings of any special interest, and not much to be had in the way of amusement.

A great deal of fighting took place in Uva in the old days. The Portuguese were mercilessly slaughtered when they attempted to get into that part of the world, and the British lost many men before the proud Sinhalese submitted to their rule. There are still military posts and abandoned forts to be seen here and there, but the country is now very quiet and peaceful, and in the villages scattered about the Natives are unsophisticated, simple, and kindly.

Badulla lies low, at the base of a noble mountain

(Namunucoola) with a broad river flowing near. In its streets, which are wide and shaded by graceful inga samen and other trees, are a good many Native shops. Some of them contain the different fruits which grow so well in that part of the Island—unusually large pineapples, guavas, grenadillas, rambutans, huge green jak fruit, etc. Others have a collection of strange vegetables: bandakai, brinjals, vivid red chillies, avocada pears, and insipid bread-fruit; or they may display ingredients for curry making; piles of snowy rice, coco-nuts, Bombay duck, popodums, and so on. There are odd looking cakes, too, called "hoppers," made of coco-nut milk and rice flour; pottery of artistic shapes; tawdry jewellery—the medley of things always to be seen where Natives congregate.

The bungalows in the little town are festooned with brilliant creepers of blue, magenta, crimson, and yellow—a mixture of colours that would jar in an English garden, but somehow seem all right in the brilliant sunshine of the East. There are several buildings that are interesting, notably the Kacheri, or Court, which is built on the site of the palace in which a Prince of Uva once lived.

In the pretty little English Church there is a memorial to a Major Rodgers, who was indeed a mighty hunter in his day, for no fewer than fifteen hundred elephants are said to have been shot by him. He escaped all sorts of dangers, only to be killed in the end by a flash of lightning. Outside, in the old cemetery, a slab of stone, with an inscription to the memory of a certain Sophia Wilson, has gradually become embedded in the trunk of a Bo tree, which has lifted it completely off the ground,

TAPPING RUBBER

The modern one-cut system of tapping rubber is now much used in Ceylon. The workers are seen here making the necessary incision in the trees.

and holds it in a tight embrace. The superstitious Natives look on it with considerable awe, convinced the gods must have greatly favoured one whose memory is so enshrined in the most sacred of all trees.

Badulla has a specially good Rest House, and a Club where "The merry men of Uva" meet, and live up to their pleasant title. Many of them come from remote bungalows, which, even in these days of motors, must often be lonely, and few of the "Sine Dorais" (literally "Little Masters," used by Natives in adressing all young Europeans) can afford the luxury of a car. There is every excuse for them if they make merry when they meet, and they never, by any chance, miss the opportunity

The Race Course has a pleasing situation in the valley, with Botanical Gardens near. In the river Natives can usually be seen, standing in the water and pouring it from chatties, or pots, over their heads—their method of bathing; or just sitting about "sumah," an expressive Tamil word often used by Europeans. It means doing nothing in particular, simply existing, in fact—no more and no less! On the wide roads that lead to some of the estates, carts drawn by patient bullocks may be moving along, their drivers apparently fast asleep, for it takes endless shouting and tooting of motor-horns before they can be induced to get out of the way of other vehicles. Funny little hooded carts (that remind one of those described in *Kim*) jog by—packed with chattering Natives, who bulge with many mysterious bundles. They are usually going on a visit to some distant Temple.

Paddy—or rice—grows well in the neighbourhood of Badulla. The lovely jade green terraces lie, tier above tier, on the steep mountain sides. Natives may be scattering the seeds (literally "casting their bread upon the waters") or great clumsy buffaloes, harnessed to the most primitive of ploughs, may be turning the furrows. The Sinhalese believe that the success or otherwise of their crops is entirely "on the lap of the gods," therefore everything possible must be done to propitiate them. For this reason, many curious rites are gone through in connection with rice growing.

Before beginning to clear the land an Astrologer is consulted. He announces the date on which operations may confidently be started, suggests some one not afflicted with "the evil eye" to begin the work of preparing the ground, and even indicates which buffaloes should be employed to tramp the weeds and tread the damp soil.

The sowing of the seed is attended with considerable ceremony, and many incantations. When the tiny plants appear, charms of various kinds are used to scare away the devils, or anything of a more prosaic nature, such as "poochies" (insects, etc.), likely to injure them. Often in passing rice fields at this stage, a low crooning may be heard; it is someone reciting the story of Buddha's goodness in keeping all evil from the growing rice. When the first sickle is used on the ripe grain, there is great rejoicing; drums are beaten, tom-toms thumped, and devil dancers career about making fearsome noises. The women, later, carry the sheaves on their heads to the threshing floor, where a peculiar rite is gone through.

In the middle of the floor a series of circles has been traced with ashes, and divided into sections.

NEAR NUWARA ELIJA

A typical view of the wild, grand country in the neighbourhood of Nuwara Elija.

On those have been drawn different objects: a relic of Buddha, a conch shell, lotus flower, bird, or snake, etc. Towards those objects the bearer of the first sheaf (someone with a reputation for being lucky has been carefully chosen) walks with dignity. She goes, slowly, three times round the circles, making a low obeisance each time, then, with a quick movement, she throws her sheaf on the particular object on the sections which the Astrologer has declared to be the most auspicious, and makes a profound salaam to it before retiring. Three other women follow, and go through exactly the same performance, leaving their sheaves on the top of the first. The others are then at liberty to place theirs where they choose.

In the evening buffaloes are brought to the threshing floor and driven over the grain, while the Natives present sing—or rather chant, special verses suited to the occasion. Winnowing and pounding take place later, accompanied by more incantations, before the grain is finally stored in the granaries.

The Sinhalese are wonderfully clever in keeping their fields supplied with the necessary water, every stream being deflected for the purpose, and aqueducts, sometimes of the most primitive kind, made of bamboos which serve as pipes, convey the liquid to the different terraces. The buffaloes, so dangerous in their wild state, are, when tamed, remarkably tractable with Natives, and quite small Sinhalese boys are able to manage them without difficulty. It is wiser, however, for Europeans to give those animals a wide berth, for they are capable of being decidedly unpleasant with strangers.

"Beef Box" Coolies

Occasionally, in going along a cart-road, one or two tame elephants may be seen moving solemnly along, their drivers addressing them, now and again, in a peculiar wheedling tone, almost as if talking to naughty children. On the narrow, steep roads that generally lead to bungalows on tea estates, coolies may be carrying a chair, strapped on two poles, on their shoulders. In it some European lady, too timid to ride, and unable to manage the climb on foot, is seated. She is being conveyed out to tea or tiffin.

On certain days of the week a string of coolies, carrying battered tin boxes on their heads, may be observed, wending its way to the different estates. They are full of importance, and so they ought to be, for are they not "Beef Box" coolies, entrusted with the rather tough beef, goat masquerading as mutton, minute eggs, etc., on which their august "Dorais" are to be fed? Other important coolies are those known as "Tappuls": they carry letters once each day to the different bungalows, and are always sure of a welcome, more especially on "home mail" night.

In a very secluded spot, hidden from the vulgar gaze by many trees, one sees a large Native house which, obviously, belongs to some Sinhalese of position. It is the home of the Ratamahatmaya—or chief Native Headman of the district. The writer was, on one occasion, invited to take tea inside, and was most courteously received by the Ratamahatmaya and his graceful, dark-eyed wife. The house was furnished in a rather bizarre fashion, hideous modern little tables with cheap ornaments on them, ugly cane chairs and common china, being

THE MORNING BATH

The elephant has just had his early tub, & is in good humour as a consequence. His Mahout seems to be in a precarious position, but knows he is safe, for the huge animal is perfectly docile.

mixed with really beautiful carved ebony and satin wood furniture. There were several oddly shaped basins of copper and silver, vases and lamps of unusual and artistic design adorned with gods and goddesses, and charming old brass "betel" boxes. All of those things were badly in need of cleaning, and were certainly not seen to advantage, as they were arranged with no sort of order, some of them even lying on the handsome Indian rugs with which the floor was covered.

After a few minutes of rather constrained conversation, the Ratamahatmaya led the way to a large, bare room which had a faint odour of jasmine and roses. A long, low table was arranged for tea, and decorated with different kinds of flowers and ferns. The hostess, looking a perfect picture in her yellow silk draperies and soft white bodice trimmed with lace, stood humbly on one side; it is not etiquette for a Sinhalese woman to sit at table with her husband. The tea was strong, and so intensely sweet that it was difficult to swallow; the fact that the cup was half filled with goat's milk did not help matters. There were quantities of little cakes covered with coloured sugar, and tasting unpleasantly of coco-nut oil. Fortunately some specially good bananas and delicious mangos were also served, and under their skins it was possible to conceal portions of those sickly cakes.

After tea—a rather protracted meal, and not exactly gay, as the Ratamahatmaya's knowledge of English was limited—the hostess asked her husband, timidly, if it would interest "Lady" to see her jewellery. It would! So a large, beautifully chased, and, incidentally, decidedly dirty silver box of Kandyan design was produced. In it there was a dazzling display of jewels; bracelets and anklets of gold studded with roughly cut emeralds; massive rings of quaint design; long chains sparkling with rubies and sapphires, and delicate filigree work. The jewellery was badly kept, but some of the old pieces were most covetable, and must have been of great value.

It was difficult to keep up a conversation with the Ratamahatmaya's wife, as her English was confined to three words—"Yes," "Please," "Lady"—those were repeated at intervals, with a charming smile, but got a trifle monotonous. Her husband, who must have seen that both hostess and guest were becoming exhausted, came to the rescue, and suggested a visit to his elephants. Those were found below in an enclosure and were put through various antics, kneeling down on one knee; making salaams; catching bananas thrown to them, etc. The scene, with the elephants grouped under the tall palms, the brilliant sun shimmering through branches of oleander trees covered with pink blossoms; the orange and lime trees laden with golden fruit, and waving bamboos, was typically Oriental. Two Buddhist priests in their yellow robes stood discreetly at a distance, a few old retainers in white and cherry coloured garments of an antique pattern hovered round the portly Ratamahatmaya, and several bright faced Sinhalese children, in their birthday suits, stood perilously near the great animals. But there was no need for fear, the elephants knew them all, and were absolutely to be trusted.

The Ratamahatmayas have no longer the same

power in Ceylon as in days gone by; they have, however, an air of superiority—a certain swagger, that always marks them from the common herd, and when, on special occasions, they appear in public in their full costume, they look most imposing. It is not surprising to find that the humbler Sinhalese treat them with great respect, and as a rule those Native Headmen are exceedingly kind and considerate, to those of lower birth than themselves.

CHAPTER VIII

LIFE ON A TEA ESTATE

" Variety is the spice of life."

THE riding paths on the side of Namunacoola (which, translated, means " the hill of the gods ") lead through tea bushes that are sheltered from the winds of the monsoon by belts of grevillea trees—on to the different bungalows. Those are placed at a considerable distance apart; they are low, one storey buildings with wide, open verandahs, and have pretty, well-cared-for gardens. The life in all of them is much the same, except that the " Peria Dorai " (big master), that is to say, the owner or manager of an estate can, and does, allow himself more in the way of luxury than his " Sine Dorais," or assistants.

At dawn, a very beautiful time in Ceylon, when the sky is tinted with rose and gold, and the fresh, sweet scent of flowers is blown in at the open windows by a gentle breeze, the " Boy " knocks, rather sharply in case his summons is ignored, and leaves the early tea and some fruit in the dressing-room. If the Peria Dorai is feeling energetic he will get up to attend Muster, but is more likely to leave that to his Sine Dorai and " Creepers," and begin his own work after breakfast. That meal over, he goes to his office to look through his correspondence ; give his clerks their orders for the day ; or listen to " coolie " grievances, should there be any.

Meanwhile the Dorasanie (mistress of the house if the planter happens to be a married man) goes to her store-room, discusses menus, and gives out supplies to her skilful Sinhalese cook. Her next duty is to write what is known as the " Beef Book," in which all her needs in the way of provisions are noted. It may be returned with some cryptic message, scribbled on it in impossible English, or—as once happened when brains were ordered—with the startling anouncement from the butcher: " Very sorry, Lady, no brains at all to be found in this town ! "

Some women in Ceylon never go to their kitchens, fearing they may see things calculated to take away their appetites, but most insist on making a daily inspection. The kitchen coolie, who is the cook's right hand, may, if left to himself, have primitive notions of cleanliness (he *has* been known to strain coffee through an old sock) and, when new to office, may think his " Lady's " requirements purely fantastic; but after a time he begins to realize the advantage of a clean, bright kitchen, and when he gets to that stage, all is well.

Domestic duties over—they are very light, for servants are numerous and generally quite good—the Dorasanie wanders round the garden, cutting flowers generously. They grow in abundance, but have to be renewed daily, as they last a sadly short time in the East. What a blaze of colour there is !—bright blue " morning glory," pink camellias, purple and red bougainvilleas, scarlet salvias, golden alamandas and abutilons, hibiscus of many hues, and brilliant crotons. There are roses too, very lovely, but with curiously little scent, and Arum and " Madonna " lilies—growing everywhere.

If her husband is still busy the Dorasanie arranges the flowers herself, if not, she hands them to the " Podian," a useful little person who takes the place, more or less, of a page boy, or under footman, in England. He was inclined at first to mix them up, regardless of colour, in one vase, and then pack them well down to the same level, but has been taught a better way, and being—like all Natives—fond of flowers, has learnt to arrange them lightly, and with considerable taste.

The horsekeepers, or grooms, dressed in white with vivid yellow sashes and turbans, having brought the ponies to the door, the Peria Dorai and Dorasanie are ready to start on a round of the estate. There may be censorious people who think that a wife ought not to accompany her husband on those occasions, but that is absurd, as, unless stupid or tactless, she never interferes with his work in any way. When he stops, as he frequently does, to give orders to his assistants, see how the coolies are getting on, or to visit the factory, she gets off her pony, finds a shady tree, and settles under it to read; to enjoy the view that never fails to charm her; or to exchange a few words, in halting Sinhalese or Tamil, with any Natives who may pass, in return for their courteous salaams.

It has been delightfully cool until, as it gets nearer noon, the sun becomes very hot, and it is wiser to return to the bungalow. There is a delightful uncertainty as to how many may sit down to tiffin and other meals ; people drop in unexpectedly, and are always sure of a welcome. Native servants like when there are guests, and take pride in showing what they can produce on short notice. Sometimes the menu, when hastily added to, is a little perplexing. " What on earth does ' Wilderness ' mean at the end of the menu ? " demanded a puzzled Dorasanie on one occasion. " That plenty good English word," explained her " Boy " rather huffily, " I looking at one dissonary, it saying desert meaning wilderness, so I putting." Then it dawned on her, obviously he had mixed up " desert " and " dessert."

Another Boy had apparently invented a new pudding with the unusual name " Continued Pudding " ; he had been trying to read an English cookery book which had " Continued " where the recipe went on over the page. It seemed quite a smart name for a pudding, so was promptly used. " Minced Pups " may not sound exactly inviting, but are harmless little puffs of mincemeat ; for some reason all Ceylon servants persist in calling puffs " pups." It was a Christian cook who once (this story has been told before, but will bear repetition) made a large, rich, and exceedingly indigestible cake, iced it, and put on the top, in pink letters, " Prepare to meet thy God " !

After tiffin, coffee, and cigarettes in the verandah, there is a brief siesta, then the Peria Dorai goes out for a short time, or finishes his correspondence, while the Dorasanie reads, writes, or does a little gardening until tea. Usually some of the young assistants and " Creepers " come in for that pleasant little meal, and tennis, or a walk follows, unless they have had a very busy day and are tired. In that case they rest in comfortable " long " chairs and talk shop, if that is not forbidden, as it sometimes has to be in case they develop into dreadful bores.

In the evening the Tappul (letter coolie) arrives, and there is just time to run through the mail, and glance at newspapers, before dressing for dinner. When that is over there may be music, billiards, or bridge (if there happens to be four) and reading, unless a stroll in the garden is preferred, to listen to the curious sounds of a tropical night; look at the twinkling stars in the cloudless sky, and the lights in the villages away below in the valley, or watch the myriads of fireflies and other insects dancing through the trees.

At new moon there is often considerable noise from the coolie lines. The Saami (or god) may be taken out from the local temple, mounted on a wonderful wooden peacock, accompanied by masked devil dancers, and the monotonous throbbing of tom-toms. Or some coolie may have suddenly become possessed by what is known as the " Demon "; in that condition he will shiver and shake, make horrible noises, and terrify the women folk, until the Perai Dorai sends a peremptory message that the one possessed must stop that noise at once otherwise he will come along and attend to the " Demon " himself! That settles the matter; the Master is kind and just, but he has singularly little patience with demons! In a short time quiet is restored.

Life on a tea estate need not be monotonous; there are always things happening that make for variety. The visits of the English Padre some-

GIANT BAMBOOS

In the Peredeniya gardens the giant bamboos grow to an incredible size. The rich colouring of their stems & delicate green of the leaves make them very arresting.

times on a Sunday (if there happens to be no church near) when a bright little service is held. It is attended by men who ride some distance to be present, and they remain to play vigorous tennis after it is over. Those services, however, have become less necessary now that so many planters possess motors. The Visiting Agent may arrive to ride round the estate, and, unless it is privately owned, to send a report of how it is progressing to interested directors in England. Then there are delightful shooting expeditions to the low country; perhaps a motor run to Nuwara Eliya, Kandy, or Colombo; the local Races to attend; and occasionally—quite an event—a visit from the Governor, when lunches, dinners, dances, etc., take place.

An amusing visitor at the bungalow is the Tamby—or peddler, usually over from India. He arrives, accompanied by one or two assistants, heavily laden with bundles. The contents of those, silks, rugs, and gay curtains from Kashmir, brasses, elaborate gold and silver embroideries on cheap satin, lace, etc., are strewn all over the verandah floor, and lively bargaining follows. He is a soft-spoken, plausible fellow the Tamby, and even when he tosses a rupee to decide a price (as he loves to do) he always seems to come off best in the end.

A less popular visitor is the Dhoby, who appears more or less regularly. His appalling method of beating the most fragile laces or muslins on stones, just as he does stronger materials, has a disastrous effect. Those things are brought back in a sadly dilapidated condition at times, though he tries to hide it by adroit folding. The Ayah, who "maids" the Dorasanie, is never deceived. She shakes out each garment contemptuously, giving the Dhoby some idea of the scorn she feels for himself, and his relations for several generations back, till a scandalized mistress interferes, implores the Dhoby to mend his ways (perfectly conscious she is asking the impossible) and sends her Ayah, still muttering angrily, to some other work.

A visit from the Native tailor is also rather trying. He invariably arrives several days after he has been expected, squats on the floor with his antiquated machine, and proceeds to give his surprising ideas on the latest "fassens." He has made up his mind, quite definitely, on the subject, and if he has, for example, decided that big tucks are the "fassen," nothing an exasperated Dorasanie can say will induce him to make small ones. It is useless trying to oppose him, for all Native tailors were born stubborn, and it is well to give in gracefully. He can sew, there is that to be said for him—and he is a picturesque figure in his yellow and red garments, with his turban bristling with pins and needles, as he sits crosslegged; also the Ayah likes him, and will be particularly amiable while he is in the bungalow.

And then there is Christmas, when there may be as many as twenty young men staying, for a couple of days, in the bungalow, some of them sleeping at night on mattresses hastily put down on the verandah floor by the domestics—but the Dorais are happy and gay, and make light of any small discomfort. They play tennis and other games until the light fails, then, after a dinner which always includes the orthodox turkey and plum pudding, no matter how hot the weather may be, play bridge or billiards, and end by singing "Auld Lang Syne"—just a little huskily, because they are thinking of their people keeping Christmas far away in England.

There is a string of Natives coming and going to the bungalow on Christmas Day, and they enjoy seeing their Dorais at play. Sometimes their gifts are rather embarrassing, as when the writer had three entire sides of goat, and two large bottles of extremely bad whisky presented to her. Other gifts on that same morning consisted of three loaves of bread, some sugary biscuits, a parcel of sticky dates, several coco-nuts, highly coloured Native sweets, and a huge packet of fireworks! Fortunately servants are obliging, and have endless relations, so such gifts can be dealt with satisfactorily—when the kind donors are at a safe distance.

Of course life varies on different estates, not only according to the part of the Island in which the planters live, but also according to their individual tastes and, incidentally, their incomes. Grey days come, even in beautiful Ceylon, in the monsoon for example. The sun then disappears behind banks of dark clouds, the torrential rain patters pitilessly against the window panes, and a ghostly mist creeps in at each crack and cranny, making everything damp and clammy. It is impossible on some days to venture out at all, even the coolies remain in their lines, huddled under the sacks they pull over their heads. But if sometimes a little dreary, there are compensations. It is pleasant to sit by a blazing fire of logs, to have extra leisure for reading, and, in the delightful intervals when the sun appears, to go out riding or walking in the cool, fresh air.

Thunderstorms, which are of frequent occurrence in Ceylon, more especially during the monsoons, are on a majestic scale. The play of the vivid lightning, flashing over the mountain sides, and the crash of the thunder as it rolls and reverberates from peak to peak, is an awesome, never-to-be-forgotten experience.

In the Sine Dorais' bungalows there is, naturally, a little less luxury than in those of the older men, and their lives, at times, must be just a little lonely and dull. But they are always made welcome at their Peria Dorai's and other bungalows; they have the races, polo, tennis, football, cricket, etc., to break the monotony from time to time; and they can look forward to a long vacation in England, after a few years. Their servants, often inexperienced, can be decidedly trying, and, as a rule, there is no Dorasanie to keep them in order. They mean well, but are capable of doing the most unexpected things. One Sine Dorai, who was going to entertain some lady friends, told his Tamil "Boy" that he wished him to make his bungalow as nice as possible for the occasion. In his verandah were three head of elk of which he was rather proud, having shot them himself. To his horror, on returning from work the day his friends were expected, he found the heads painted a bright blue! The "Boy," amazed at his Master's quite unforeseen wrath, mildly explained that he had been making the bungalow "plenty nice for the Dorasanies." He had found a large pot of blue paint (bought to renew the outside of a bath) and had the brilliant idea that it would smarten up the elks' heads!

When the ladies arrived they found their host suffering from the Blues (in more senses than one!), but it was a hilarious little party that sat down to tiffin, and the "Boy" added to the merriment by having carefully written on the menu "only four snipe," his delicate way of hinting that, as there were five people at table, one must pass that dish!

There is a sad tale told of one young man who, having occasion to go into his kitchen, saw a small, naked brown baby sitting on what looked like a round piece of dark wood. "Where did you find that piece of wood, Boy?" he demanded, after patting the child's head. "That not one piece of wood, Dorai," replied the domestic in some surprise, "that only the salted beef for Master's dinner." Let us hope this last story is a libel, for those Boys are not always as black as they are painted.

CHAPTER IX

ADAM'S PEAK. THE PEARL FISHERY.

" God loves those who dare much."

ADAM'S PEAK! In all the world there is no other mountain held in such profound reverence, or that has so many strange legends connected with it. Surely no one can look at its lofty pinnacle without feeling his imagination quickened by the thought of the countless millions who, from the earliest ages, have made the laborious climb to the top, in touching confidence of saving their immortal souls.

Amongst the early Christians there was a tradition that Ceylon was the resting place found by Adam and Eve after they were expelled from Paradise; in that case their punishment does not seem to have been unduly severe! Before leaving the Island Adam is supposed to have gone to the top of the Peak, for a farewell look at the magnificent view, and to have left the " Sri Pada "—or sacred footprint—as a memento of his visit.

The Mahommedans have another tradition. According to them Adam landed on the Peak when cast out from Eden, and stood there, on one foot, until he had atoned for his sin. Strangely enough the Chinese, in some of their ancient writings, refer to the footprint as that of the " Pwankkoo " or first man. The Hindus, however, declare that it was the god Siva who left the impression; the Buddhists insist that it was Buddha, when on his last visit to Ceylon; while one of the primitive writers dogmatically asserts that it was no other than the Devil! It is a mystery never likely to be solved; but of one thing we can be quite sure, it is not the footprint of any mortal, for it happens to be five feet long, and broad in proportion.

Every year, to this day, thousands of pilgrims make the wearisome climb to the top of the Peak to pay humble homage to the "Sri Pada," and it is greatly to the credit of those devotees of different faiths that there is no quarrelling or dissension of any kind. It is pathetic to see some of them; old, physically weak, deformed, helped on by kindly relations and friends, and their own indomitable faith. Not a few faint by the way, some have even lost their lives by falling from the dizzy heights, but the others press on, undaunted. "It is Fate," they say with a sigh, comforted by the thought that death is well met when one is on a pious pilgrimage.

The climb can be made either from Hatton, through the fertile district of Maskeliya, or from Ratnapura—a place noted for the sapphires and other gems found in its near neighbourhood. The route by the first is nearly always chosen by Europeans and the less zealous pilgrims. The other involves greater hardship, but those who undertake it acquire more merit, and for that reason it will always be favoured by the most devout. Let us see what it is like.

The road winds along through fine country, but is tiring from the start, as it is usually very hot in that part of the Island. The air gets cooler as one ascends, and the richly tropical vegetation gives place to rather stunted trees, juniper, crimson rhododendrons, and plants only to be found at a high altitude. Sometimes the road skirts the very edge of a deep abyss; at one point the pilgrims invariably pause—it is the spot where a poor maiden fell over into the yawning gulf below. Her spirit, so they say, still haunts the place, and as they call her name " Nilihela " it is returned faintly. If it is hinted that it is only an echo they are incredulous, and go on, in the belief that they have heard the sad voice of the unfortunate, but meritorious Nilihela, who disappeared so long ago.

For the greater part of the way the Peak is entirely hidden, but at last, after a toilsome climb, it comes into view. Shortly after the pilgrims stop, to go through certain rites and purification at a sacred stream which trickles from the mountain. According to one of the many fables connected with this stream, its waters come direct from the sea, but are without any trace of salt, and if invalids drink of them, all illness vanishes, as though by magic. Be that as it may, the stream certainly seems to have a beneficial effect on the pilgrims, for after their purification they continue the hard climb with renewed vigour, repeating monotonously, but with fervour " *Saadu, Saadu* " (Amen) as they go.

The road as it gets nearer the top becomes increasingly difficult, and the rocks are so precipitous that it seems impossible they can ever be scaled. At one place there is a cliff with a summit that overhangs the path; it would be hopeless to attempt

COCOA TREES

Workers are busy picking the red and golden pods of cocoa which they pile in their wicker baskets.

going on were it not for an iron ladder and chains that have been fixed to the rock for those ascending to hold on by, as they make their perilous progress. There are ten chains in all, rusty and ill-shaped. How they and the ladder were ever fastened to the rock is a problem that has baffled all who have ever tried to solve it.

About the chains on Adam's Peak there are many fantastic stories told. One is that Adam put the topmost—known as "the chain of witness," in position, with his own hands! Another is that when Alexander the Great visited Ceylon (or "Serendib" as it was called in his day), he gave orders that the ladder and chains should be attached to the rock, to enable him to pay homage to the sacred footprint. This was immediately done, though by what means history does not relate. A Persian poet (Ashreef) in one of his compositions describes in picturesque language the coming of Alexander the Great to the Island, and his pilgrimage to Adam's Peak. He mentions the chains that were then riveted to the rock, "that travellers might climb the mountain and so attain glory." There can be no question as to their antiquity; their rusty, clumsily made links bear the marks of great age.

As the pilgrims cling to the rough chains they murmur some invocation to their gods, never daring to look down from the giddy height, for a sudden vertigo, or unexpected gust of wind, would end all hope of their longed-for goal, the "Sri Pada." One can just imagine their intense relief when at last, on a small platform, under a canopy, but unconcealed from view, they see the sacred footprint. Is their faith just a little shaken as they look at that rough outline of a gargantuan foot ? If so, they never show it. Very reverently they put down their offerings of flowers, bowing low several times, and repeating interminably "*Saadu, Saadu.*" Their worship ends when they have struck an ancient bell, and drunk of a sacred stream near the summit. They may then, if they will, look from the Peak to where " hills peep o'er hills and Alps on Alps arise "—a marvellous panorama, for the view is superb.

Next morning at dawn (a certain number stop over night and must suffer from the intense cold at that height) the pilgrims may see, if weather conditions permit, that strange phenomenon—the shadow of Adam's Peak, a ghost-like duplicate of the mountain. But perhaps they are too much absorbed by the thought that they are on such holy ground to be surprised at anything, no matter how unusual. They begin the descent quickly, their faces lit by the happiness of a duty done, and they show wonderfully little sign of fatigue. One wonders whether they ever find any of the gems, poetically called " Adam's Tears," which were once supposed to have been strewn along the path—but perhaps those jewels have long since vanished.

Hatton, from which the easier route is taken to the Peak, is in a district where there are many flourishing tea estates. There is a good hotel provided for those wishing to undertake the climb from there, and it is possible to motor, or drive, for a considerable part of the way, the climb not beginning till Oosmalle, which is about three miles from the summit. It is a tiring walk, and none too

A BUDDHIST TEMPLE ON ADAM'S PEAK

The little temple shown here is visited by all Buddhist pilgrims & frequently by those of other faiths.

easy in parts, but chains, similar to those on the other route, are a help at the more difficult places, and it is certainly worth some fatigue to see a spot so steeped in tradition, and with a view of such unusual beauty.

We have seen some of the Natives in pious mood, let us glance at them engaged in a purely mundane matter—the Pearl Fishery. For over three thousand years that has taken place in Ceylon in a small bay, by the Gulf of Manaar and near the Moddragam River, on the north-west coast. A town springs up, mushroom-like, for the occasion, and vanishes at the end of the fishery; it has the impossible name of Marichchukkaddi.

A suitable date, for the beginning of the Pearl Fishery, is only decided after a careful inspection of the oyster beds has been made, and it has been roughly calculated how many oysters are likely to have reached the stage required. Directly there seems a chance of a successful fishery, the day on which it will commence is announced, and the news spreads like wildfire all over Ceylon, to India, Burma, and elsewhere. Within an incredibly short time thousands, sometimes as many as forty to fifty, have hurried to the spot, all keenly desirous of taking part in such a thrilling game of chance.

Streets are laid out, bungalows hastily built to accommodate officials and others. There are Rest Houses for visitors, huts for the more humble folk; a Post and Telegraph Office, Hospital, indeed everything likely to be wanted for the comfort of all concerned. The fleet of pearlers, some three hundred boats of varying types, is drawn up in line, and moored to the beach. They make a charming picture as they lie in wait for the signal to begin operations. That comes at midnight, when the boom of a gun and banging of tom-toms tell that a start can be made. What a hurry and scurry there is, a shouting in Sinhalese, Tamil, Arabic and other languages, as each boat makes a frantic effort to get off first. After they have all departed there is perfect stillness, as if everyone in the town is waiting, breathlessly, for the result.

The divers go down, some head—but the majority feet—foremost. They remain under water from forty seconds to a minute, rapidly filling their baskets with oysters. When they give the signal the man who is holding the rope by which they were let down, immediately pulls them up. The work goes on until the boats get a warning from the shore that the fishing for that day is over, then a most exciting race follows. All are intensely eager to get in to the market as quickly as possible, knowing that high prices can be got from those buyers impatient to see at once what the first oysters are like. Before anyone is allowed to land, police board each boat, and search thoroughly in case any pearls may have already been found and concealed. The divers are said to be exceedingly clever in hiding them, and the police have to be very much on the alert, as well as impervious to temptation, for bribery is by no means unknown.

There are several sheds arranged on the beach, and divided into compartments, one for the crew of each boat. After the police examination is over, the divers and others make a dash for those sheds, with their bags of oysters, and hastily divide the contents of them into three heaps, as near the same size as possible. One of those heaps is the share allotted to divers by the officials in charge. Directly it has been apportioned they take it away, and are besieged by buyers, all keen to gamble on the chance of finding pearls. Meanwhile the other heaps of oysters are counted carefully, and later in the day are put up for sale by the thousand. They are eagerly bid for, but the most thrilling time comes next morning, when the oysters are opened and pearls are found—or the reverse! What commotion and excitement there is, and, sometimes, what bitter disappointment. It is a most unpleasant operation the opening of oysters, and the odour is hateful—it seems almost impossible to believe that anything so lovely as a pearl could come from such an ugly setting of dirt and debris—but it does! Sometimes one of great value is found, and then there is much rejoicing, and warm congratulations to the lucky finder.

The Pearl Fishery provides a constant sensation for the three to six weeks during which it lasts. Natives dearly love a gamble, and Europeans are almost, if not quite, as eager. Within the last few years the Government has leased the Fishery, at a high rental, to "The Ceylon Company of Pearl Fishing," who have now all rights of this interesting and lucrative trade.

CHAPTER X

GALLE. MATARA. NATIVES EN FÊTE

" By verdant groves and the edge of crystal waters."

THE deep blue waters of the Bay of Galle ripple over golden sands, or throw up masses of silvery spray, on the fortified rocks which protect its harbour. Palms bend their graceful heads on its shores, and the surrounding hills are dark with forest trees, Adam's Peak standing out, sharply outlined, against a cloudless sky.

Was it really from this quiet bay that ships once sailed away with a fascinating cargo of " gold and silver, ivory, apes, and peacocks," destined for the great King Solomon ? It may be so, for according to more than one historian there is reason to believe that Galle was the Tarshish of the Scriptures. The thought certainly adds to the glamour and romance that seem to cling to the place.

As one stands under the shade of the swaying palms, it is not difficult to conjure up a vision of far away days, when curious craft of every description, manned by swarthy mariners, all eager to procure some of the treasures to be found in fair Serendib, put into the little bay, not without danger from the rocks and uncertain currents. The Sabeans, Persians, Greeks, Romans, and Egyptians all came at various times we are told,

THE OLD DUTCH GATE AT GALLE

The old gate is in excellent preservation, as can be seen. It is shown here from the outside.

and it was at the busy port of Galle that the Arabians met the picturesque junks of the Chinese, and filled their vessels with jewels, spices, and other luxuries, to carry back to Bassora (or Basra as we know it) in the golden days of Haroun-al-Raschid. The enchanting tales of The Arabian Nights flash back to one's memory, especially those of Sindbad the Sailor who, it may be remembered, was supposed to have been wrecked on his way to Serendib, with gifts to the king of that favoured isle. The Natives in those days (so Tennent tells us in his delightful book on Ceylon) were believed by many of their visitors to be demons, or evil spirits. Possibly the reason for this belief was the strange habit they had of keeping out of sight. They used to steal out at dusk, and place their wares where they could be found, returning later to collect whatever goods had been left in exchange.

Until comparatively recent times the Veddahs (or aborigines—now almost extinct) continued this strange practice. The writer, some years ago, in an out-of-the-way corner of the Island, saw about a dozen of those Veddahs. They were weird, wild-looking beings, unreclaimed from savage life, wearing no clothing except a scrap of loin cloth, and carrying primitive bows and arrows. Their tangled black hair fell in wisps over their unintelligent faces, and they never smiled or talked amongst themselves, giving only a kind of grunt, by way of thanks, when some trifling gifts were offered to them. Of recent years they have become much more civilized, and no longer stick rigidly to their ancient customs ; they have intermarried with the Sinhalese, so that it is now almost impossible to distinguish them from the lower caste Natives—but this is a digression.

The Portuguese in their time, the Dutch, and later the British, all put in at Galle, but the construction of the breakwater in Colombo, which provides safe anchorage for shipping of any size, no matter what the weather conditions may be, has meant that mail and passenger steamers, as well as other important vessels, now use that port entirely. It is true that Galle has lost much of its former prosperity, but it still has a lure of its own. Its streets, shaded by lovely Suriya trees, studded with exquisite primrose blossoms that turn to purple as they fade, are delightfully quiet. The houses, mostly of Dutch architecture, look cool and pleasant in their setting of palms and flowers, and the Native bazaars show some of the tortoise-shell, and other delicate work, for which Galle was once famous. There are a few modern shops, offices, etc., and the hotel is roomy and comfortable, also the golf course is good, and there is a fine open space for games of all sorts. The old Dutch Church, in use to this day, is worth seeing, as it has several monuments and tombs of interest. A picturesque, though now dismantled fort, encloses the town; it has a quaint old gateway, typically Dutch. But when all is said and done, it is the ghost of the past which haunts the place that appeals most strongly, at least to those who happen to be blessed with an imagination.

The drives and motor runs along the sea coast are fascinating, more especially late in the day, when the sky is often splashed with the gorgeous colouring of an Eastern sunset. Curious catamarans and other Native craft may be seen, drawn up on the beach, their scantily clad owners looking like so many bronze figures as they loiter near them. Sometimes one catches a glimpse of the day's catch, queer uncommon fish of varied tints, with scales that scintillate like jewels. And the ubiquitous coco-nut palm is growing everywhere, at times bending over as if listening to the murmur of the sea. Its uses are so many that it is only possible to mention a few.

Natives, almost invariably, build their huts and hollow out their canoes from the trunk of the coco-nut palm. Round the patch of ground near their homes, in which they grow limes, oranges, plaintains, etc., they put a fence made with the stalks of the leaves. From the fibre they weave mats, baskets, and other useful things of the kind; in their little lamps (made from coco-nut shells) they burn the oil expressed from the kernel, or they use it on their bodies if ill, and to add brilliancy to their thick black hair. The milk of the nut makes a refreshing drink—"toddy," a sort of mild wine much liked by all Natives, is made from the sap. When fermented it becomes the more intoxicating spirit called arrack. Jaggery, the sugar that can be procured form the nut, is used in cooking, the kernel being valuable as a food, or—when dried—as copra. If there is a birth—or death—in a Sinhalese house, a piece of coco-nut blossom will generally be found there; it serves the useful purpose of keeping evil spirits at a safe distance! No wonder that the possession of even one of those precious palms is said to insure its owner against any fear of want.

Matara

A little over twenty miles, to the east of Galle, is the pleasing little town of Matara. It has the remains of a Dutch fort, and at one time did an active trade in spices. Dondra Head, the most southern point in the Island, is only a few miles farther along the coast. It was there that a Hindu temple, dedicated to Vishnu, once stood. The building, we are told, was so immense that at a distance it gave the impression of being an entire city; its roof was of copper that shone like gold, and all its ornaments were of the most gorgeous description. It shared the same fate as the Temple of a Thousand Columns, being destroyed by the Portuguese. A few " moonstone " steps, part of an ornamental parapet on which mythical animals are carved, and an odd-looking basin, are practically all that is left of its former grandeur. It is still a place of pilgrimage, however, and by devout Hindus its site is considered holy ground.

Frequently, when going along a road in Ceylon, one notices a carpet of what looks like snow; the pods of the Katu Imbul (or cotton tree) have split open, and showered their dainty white contents on the ground. Or the carpet may be of a delicate green; in that case it will suddenly become alive as one gets nearer, and resolve itself into a whirl of gay little butterflies, that flutter off in every direction. In passing through villages one often comes across charming arches, made of giant bamboos and decorated with different fruits and flowers. The Sinhalese call them " Pandals " and erect them for special occasions, to welcome some important Government official perhaps, or if there is going to be a wedding. Sometimes there are a few words

COCO-NUT PALMS

Coco-nut palms love the sea. Tall & gaunt, they fringe its shores. The Sinhalese declare coco-nuts are never happy if away from the sound of the waves.

of greeting on them: the parents of one bride even went so far, proud of their knowledge of the English language, as to put in very ornate letters: "God bless the weeded pair!" But usually there is nothing to mar the simple elegance of those graceful arches.

A Sinhalese wedding always causes great excitement in a village. The date on which it is arranged to take place is that shown as most auspicious on the horoscopes of the prospective bride and bridegroom, for Natives never undertake anything of importance without first consulting an Astrologer. Let us see what happens at the ceremony, which is held in the bride's home.

In the principal room a series of arches has been built; they are of bamboos decorated with young coco-nut palm leaves, etc., and are placed round a raised platform on which are two seats. The bridegroom arrives first, accompanied by his nearest relations, and is welcomed at the door—very ceremoniously—by those of the bride, who conduct him to his place under the archways. The happy maiden then appears, dressed very simply and attended by her parents, who lead her to the place beside the bridegroom. Directly she is seated several young girls from one of the Buddhist schools begin to sing various stanzas from the sacred books. They have high pitched, rather strident voices, and the sounds they produce are not exactly melodious.

The singing continues for some time, and when it is over the bridegroom presents his bride with—oddly enough—her wedding dress, and as much jewellery as he, and his family, can afford. She immediately retires to her room, to return shortly in all the glory of her new garment, and sparkling with as much of the jewellery as she can conveniently wear. Another stanza, specially suitable for the occasion, is then sung, and while it is going on, an elderly person of importance ties the right thumbs of the bride and bridegroom together, and continues solemnly pouring water on them (the thumbs) until the singing ends. When it does, the bridegroom unties the string, and the couple are then considered to be man and wife. They remain seated until their parents have given them their blessing—usually in the form of a short stanza of a religious nature—and they have received congratulations from others present. Then the bridegroom prepares a handful of betel and areca nut, which he presents to the bride, and she, kneeling down, humbly offers it to the most prominent person present, the whole party afterwards, with a due regard to precedence, being offered betel before they move into the room where the wedding feast is waiting.

A large table has been prepared, and is laden with curious looking cakes, rich sweets, fruits, etc. It is entirely covered by a huge white cloth, and it is not until every guest has been seated that the family Dhoby—of all people!—formally removes this cloth, and the meal begins. At up-to-date weddings there is now an ornate wedding cake, which the bride cuts in orthodox fashion. The feasting seems to go on interminably; the heat and pungent scent of temple flowers with which the room is decorated make the atmosphere stifling. One feels very sorry for the poor bride, who sits, smiling bravely, by the side of a man she scarcely knows—her husband. It is not until the Astrologer has announced that the propitious hour has come, that the young couple are allowed to go to their own home, and it is quite possible they may have to wait until another day dawns before being able to leave the parental roof.

The Sinhalese have several festivals during the year, when they wake up from their usual *dolce far niente* existence, and make quite merry. The two principal are held at the beginning of the year. At a certain hour, before the first festival commences, a gun is fired to intimate that no cooking must be done, fires must be extinguished, work and play stopped, and the time given up to meditation. A second shot makes it known that a new year has begun, and immediately there is great rejoicing. Fires are relit and special meals prepared ; offerings are taken to the Temple ; visits paid and received ; there is a banging of tom-toms, whizzing of fire-works, and general commotion. The festival lasts from two to three days (as Europeans uncomfortably realize !), special hours being appointed for certain duties, including that of taking the first bath of the year !

Wesak is held in commemoration of the day on which Buddha was born ; on the same date he is supposed to have received enlightenment and, later, to have reached Nirvana. The day is spent in bedecking his shrine in the different temples with flowers ; in doing kindly acts likely to help towards the acquirement of merit ; and in various forms of amusement.

A minor festival, but one strictly observed by both the Sinhalese and Tamils, is the ear boring ceremony. At the stage when a child is to begin wearing ear-rings an Astrologer is consulted, and informs the parent which date is likely to be a lucky one for the event to take place. Immediately invitations (which take the form of betel, and a verbal message) are sent out to relations and friends. When the day has come and the guests have assembled, a goldsmith arrives with ear-rings of gold or silver; those have sharp ends to which is attached a jewel, or—in the case of poor parents—a flower. The child has to be seated on the knee of an uncle (or someone representing that relation) and the goldsmith, after marking the ears first with lime, proceeds to bore them, and carefully fix in the ear-rings. Betel, and refreshments as various as the parents can afford, are handed to the guests, who all present gifts to the child, and make their salaams before leaving. In the case of Tamils there is a curious custom. The uncle is expected to give a goat, and to show the parents that he has brought one really worthy of their child, he gets on its back as he reaches the house where the ear boring ceremony is to take place, and appears—riding what often proves an exceedingly refractory mount!

NATIVES HARVESTING

Natives at work in the fields in the interior of Ceylon. They like harvest-time & can frequently be heard singing in high, rather quavery voices over their work.

CHAPTER XI

AN ELEPHANT KRAAL

" Peaceful, beneath primeval trees, that cast their ample shade . . . Leans the huge elephant."

WILD elephants are still very numerous in Ceylon, and a kraal, which takes place about every five years, is always looked forward to with eagerness by Europeans and Natives alike. It is held in a selected part of the jungle, and is for the purpose of capturing wild elephants, which are afterwards tamed and used on certain ceremonial occasions: for working on the roads; or they may be shipped to India and elsewhere.

The Ratamahatmayas and other Headmen decide the date and place at which a kraal will be held, and ten days or so before the time fixed they send out Native Beaters, sometimes as far afield as fifty to sixty miles, to surround and drive in the elephants to a given centre. A strong stockade is erected, enclosing a large space in the jungle, and care is taken to conceal it as much as possible, more especially near the opening through which, later, the wild elephants will be driven in. Platforms are built with accommodation for the Governor (who nearly always attends), Government officials, and a large crowd of Europeans, Burghers, Sinhalese, Tamils and others, who throng to the jungle directly they know when the kraal is likely to begin.

Decoy elephants, ridden by their Mahouts, are brought inside the stockade, and start clearing away trees and shrubs, picking them up with their trunks and tossing them on the ground. All round, at intervals, Natives are stationed, and armed with guns in case of a stampede. Fires are lit to keep the elephants off, for it is known that they are afraid of fire and detest smoke, and other precautions are taken to avoid possible danger.

For some time before the kraal actually begins, everything is done rather quietly, in order that the elephants may not be scared off in the wrong direction, but immediately they are well surrounded there is perfect pandemonium. Horns, tom-toms, all sorts of Native instruments—each noisier than the other—are brought into use; guns are fired, and there is shouting, yelling, and general excitement. The wild elephants, terrified by the noise, dash about in every direction, but their frantic efforts to escape are useless. At each point they are driven nearer and nearer to the stockade, until at last they are inside, and the opening by which they have entered is at once closed.

It is quite pathetic to see the way in which, for a long time, they rush about distractedly, trying to find some way out. Hither and thither they go, utterly bewildered by the crowd, the noise, and obstacles they come across at every turn. After many fruitless attempts it seems to dawn on them that it is hopeless trying to escape, and they huddle close together, in a dejected little group.

The decoy elephants, which have been kept waiting for the right moment to arrive, now approach, trumpeting and waving their trunks, and

A TYPICAL ROAD IN THE COUNTRY

Some idea of the beauty of the roads in Ceylon is conveyed by this picture, but the wonderful colouring, the greens & reds & golds, must be left to the imagination.

encouraged by the repeated "Ur-re!" "Ur-re!" of their Mahouts—a peculiar sound which, for some odd reason, always appeals to them. They edge closer and closer to the wild elephants, until they get sufficiently near to wedge one in between two of them, and directly they have succeeded in doing this, the Mahouts slip off, very cleverly throw a noose round the hind legs of their captive, and tie it firmly to the nearest tree. This goes on until all have been secured.

The poor animals, furious at this new humiliation, struggle violently to extricate themselves, trumpeting with rage as they find it impossible, but as time goes on they become exhausted and hungry, thirsty and subdued, meekly allow themselves to be led off and taught their new duties. The decoy elephants generally behave admirably during the whole proceedings, indeed it almost seems as if they were taking an intelligent interest in all that has been aking place, and it is amusing to watch them, languidly fanning themselves with bunches of leaves during intervals in their work.

The whole scene, away in the wilds of the jungle, is a most interesting one. It is a picnic on a gigantic scale, with plenty of excitement thrown in. During the day it is usually extremely hot, a fierce sun blazing down from a blue sky with never a cloud, and the flames of the fires adding to the heat. But the Europeans present are far too absorbed in all that is going on to grumble at anything. As for the Natives, they are perfectly happy, even when clinging to the trees, to get a good view, in positions that look decidedly precarious. A kraal is a sight after their own hearts, and their presence, in their brilliant red and yellow garments, their brown faces wreathed in smiles, adds greatly to its attraction.

Occasionally there are unavoidable accidents, and what might have led to serious trouble happened at a kraal held not so very long ago. A big decoy elephant, which had been rather troublesome from the start, shortly before the end inadvertently knelt down on one of the almost extinguished fires. Feeling the hot ashes it became terrified, and tore along to a part of the stockade where many of the spectators were standing on a platform by a fence. The excited animal crashed through, as if the fence had been made of paper instead of with strong trunks of trees, threw its Mahout under a bush (he was lucky enough to escape with nothing worse than a few scratches) and made a bolt for the jungle. Fortunately the long iron chain by which it had been tied up was trailing behind, and was skilfully caught by some Natives, who gradually succeeded in pacifying the frightened animal.

Meanwhile several of the spectators had completely lost their heads, and began scattering here and there in a panic. They were alarmed in case the other decoys should take fright, but, though obviously excited, they all remained at their posts. A stockade would not be of much use if elephants understood their own strength; mercifully they are unaware of it, and will go a long way round to avoid even quite a small fence. In this case it was only one decoy which got through the fence, and though one or two people got slightly hurt in the sudden scrimmage, there were no serious consequences.

AN ELEPHANT AT WORK

The Sinhalese find their elephants most useful in carrying heavy loads. This animal is seen lifting a log cut from a Kitul palm.

Elephant Kraals

In the old days elephant kraals took place much more frequently, and were on a larger scale. Tennent tells us that from fifteen hundred to two thousand forced labourers took part in clearing the jungle, driving in the wild elephants, etc. Even now a kraal provides work for many Natives, who are paid by Government. They undertake the duties required very willingly, for Orientals seem to have a special liking for those huge animals, and are particularly good in managing them.

The Ceylon elephants are not so large as those found in Africa, seldom being higher than eight or nine feet, and comparatively few have tusks—which is unfortunate, as the Chinese are said to prefer the ivory obtained in the Island to that of any other part of the world, declaring that its tint and texture make it more beautiful when carved. The hair from the tails of elephants is so strong and wiry that it is made into bracelets by jewellers (who assure buyers that they will always be lucky if they wear them) and the teeth are sometimes made into ornaments of sorts.

The Sinhalese have several curious beliefs about elephants. One is that they live to be two, sometimes three hundred years old. Another is that, when they feel their end approaching, they retire to a peaceful valley in the mountains, not far from Adam's Peak, to die. It is interesting to read, in the *Mahawansa,* that a white elephant formed part of the retinue in one of the temples at Anuradhapura in the fifth century B.C., but it does not seem to have been looked upon as a curiosity, or treated with any special respect.

At Katugastota (near Kandy) there are a number

of elephants kept by one of the Ratamahatmayas who has his home there, near the river. It is a favourite amusement for visitors to watch them bathing, and splashing about playfully in the water. They are very docile in the hands of their Mahouts, who never seem to have the slightest fear in dealing with the big, ungainly animals. One sometimes wonders what—apart from demons and evil spirits —Natives *are* afraid of, more especially when one hears of the Sinhalese who, seeing in a local newspaper that a lightning conductor was wanted on a certain building, promptly applied for the post! After all, he knew there were conductors on tea estates, and saw no reason why he should not conduct lightning!

CHAPTER XII

SINHALESE AND TAMILS

" After all there is but one race—humanity."

SOME years ago the ordinary visitor to Ceylon was content with seeing the more important towns and their neighbourhood, as it was frequently difficult to reach, or get suitable accommodation in, the more out of the way parts of the country. Now, however, motoring has become so general that it is possible to go much farther afield, though there are still places which can only be reached by the humble bullock-cart, or on horseback, and it is to be hoped that those havens of rest and peace may be left undisturbed for a long time to come.

Besides the privately owned and other cars, there are any number of motor-lorries now to be met on most of the public roads, noisy, unpleasant things that seem altogether out of place in such beautiful surroundings. There are motor-buses too, rackety looking vehicles, vastly over-crowded, and tied up with odds and ends of string or rope, where they are falling to pieces. They are used, almost exclusively, by Natives, and the fares charged are very moderate. There is a blissful uncertainty as to when those buses will start from any point, and if it seems likely there are to be fewer passengers than usual, the chances are they will not start at all.

As one goes by car through some of the otherwise quiet little villages, dismal sounds may be heard sometimes—the owner of one of the huts has been guilty of buying a cheap, nasty gramophone, with records in the vernacular. Its strident notes jar on sensitive ears, but Sinhalese or Tamils will squat for hours listening contentedly to the same record being played over and over again.

Those village folks are very different from the partially educated, sophisticated Natives of the towns. They are poor in general, have little or no ambition, and are quite happy to live simply, and to cultivate their paddy fields as their fathers did before them. Of course the agitator is busy in Ceylon as elsewhere, stirring up trouble wherever possible, and frequently succeeding in the towns. But as a rule the villagers are apathetic where politics, or vexed questions of any kind are concerned, and on that account agitators find it more difficult to make mischief.

Sinhalese women when young are often very pretty, with clear olive skins, delicate features, and large, dreamy, brown eyes. Unfortunately, like all Orientals, they age quickly, and, as they grow old, lose much of their charm. The men are good looking, but the way in which they wear their long black hair twisted up like a woman's, gives them rather an effeminate appearance. In spite of their mild expression they flash quickly into hot anger if anything upsets them, and the knives which they carry are brought into use, sometimes on very slight provocation. Most of their quarrels are

INTERIOR OF A BUDDHIST TEMPLE

A devout little Sinhalese girl kneels before the Lord Buddha, while her mother presents a humble offering. Note the size of the warlike figure on the left.

caused, either by their women folk, or in connection with any property they may own.

Native children are attractive little things, with bright bead-like eyes and an alert expression, but they are hopelessly spoilt by their parents who make no attempt to discipline them in any way. It is always unwise to admire a Sinhalese or Tamil child when talking to its relations. " What a very plain baby," will please them far more than " What a pretty child." The reason is that they believe the gods are displeased or jealous of praise, and may vent their wrath on its object. If, on the other hand, anybody disparages one of their children, there is a pleasant feeling that the gods have been hoodwinked !

Europeans sometimes dislike having Sinhalese servants because of their too facile use of the knife, but as a matter of fact they usually behave extremely well in bungalows, becoming devoted to their " Master " and " Lady " when kindly treated, and they are more cleanly in their habits than the Tamils. Although the majority are Buddhists there are a certain number of professing Christians. They may be quite sincere, but it does not always follow that they are absolutely trustworthy. The writer remembers one Roman Catholic cook, who habitually stole the best wax candles to give to his church ! But after all, European Christians fail at times to live up to their religion, so it is hardly surprising that Native converts are not always models of virtue.

In bungalows where there are children, or where the lady of the house requires a personal maid, the Ayah is most useful. Neither Sinhalese nor

Tamil women work in any other household capacity; the rest of the work in a bungalow is done by men or boys. To her European charges the Ayah is extremely attached, and the fairer skinned the children are, the prouder will be their dusky guardian. Later on, when she marries and has children of her own, she will plaster their faces as thickly as she can with white powder, in an anxious desire that they shall look as like "Little Master" or "Little Missy" as possible. She spoils her charges shamefully, never crossing them if she can avoid it, and giving them things to eat which ought to kill them—but never does! Also she has very little regard for truth: in her opinion "the sin is not in sinning, but in the being found out." For that reason it is better for children not to be left under her care too long, even when they—and they nearly always do—love her dearly. The following story gives some idea of the difficulty in fathoming the mentality of Sinhalese of the servant class.

An English lady had found one to "maid" her who was a treasure, clean, active, a good needlewoman, and popular with the other servants. She had, however, an amiable weakness—she loved pretty things, and any object that had gold, silver, or "sparkles" had a special fascination for her. All the gold cord off an embroidered cushion in "Lady's" drawing-room was suddenly found to to have been picked off—nobody had done it of course, the Ayah being specially shocked that there should be anyone in the bungalow capable of doing such a thing. Unfortunately her mistress met her going to some special festival at the temple a few weeks later, carrying a gorgeous bag, embroidered with gold cord suspiciously like that which had disappeared from the cushion, and her eager "Please, Lady, I having this bag plenty years, long, long ago, when I very little baby," was not quite convincing.

Not long afterwards a pair of satin evening slippers, which had not been in use for some time, were required, and to their owner's dismay she discovered that all the tiny silver beads, with which the toes had been decorated, had vanished. The Ayah was sent for, and at first flatly denied that she had even seen the beads. "How then can I taking what I never seen?" she demanded with an air of injured innocence. In the end she was obliged to confess that she had taken them to sew on a small case in which she kept her betel. She was forgiven, but warned that if anything of the kind happened again, she would at once be dismissed.

The next trouble that came along was more serious. A handsome sapphire ring belonging to her mistress could not be found. It was one that its owner wore almost constantly. One morning, noticing it was not on her finger, she went to the box in which it was kept when not in use—the ring was gone! All the servants, with the exception of the Ayah, had been in the bungalow for years, and were perfectly honest. Sorrowfully "Lady" concluded her treasure must be the culprit, and asked her husband to deal with the matter. To a stern demand that she should confess her guilt the Ayah's only reply, made at intervals, was: "Please Dorai, I never taking. I not one low caste woman, I not one thief." At last her master gave his ultimatum—either she must admit having taken the ring, or he would send for the police, in either case she must go. Natives dislike anything to do with the police, and the Ayah was no exception. She thought for a minute or two, rubbing one bare foot against the other in the way her people always do when perplexed, then, with tears streaming down her cheeks, she said slowly: "Please, Dorai, I too sorry, I did taking that ring out of the little box. Then I going to take one bath in the stream, that ring have fallen off into the water and it getting lost." It sounded quite a likely story, so after a very severe reprimand, the Ayah was sent off, in dire disgrace.

But the strange thing was this—a few days later her mistress had occasion to open a drawer which was always kept locked, as it contained private papers. In turning over some of them, something that sparkled suddenly caught her eye, and—to her utter amazement—she found it was her sapphire ring. Then it flashed across her what had happened. She must have been mistaken in thinking she had not put on her ring the day she missed it, for now she remembered that just before discovering her loss, she had taken a paper out of the drawer. The ring must then have slipped off her finger (it was a trifle large as she had got thinner), fallen into the drawer, and got concealed under some of the papers.

The Ayah, who had retired to her village, was sent for, and appeared, smiling broadly. On being asked why she had said she lost the ring when bathing, she explained, not the least abashed, but evidently quite proud of the story she had invented: "Master telling he sending for the police,

THE OUTRIGGER CANOE

Very primitive, & most picturesque, these canoes are in constant use by the Sinhalese, who have used them for hundreds of years.

they plenty bad people, so I telling I have took." Her Mistress was inclined to give in to her eager request that she should be reinstalled, but "Master" was firm. She was an excellent Ayah in many ways he conceded, but there was never any knowing what particular form of mischief she would be up to next. She should be consoled for her temporary disgrace by a few rupees, and then sent back to her village.

It is a curious thing that neither Sinhalese nor Tamil women will ever mention their husband's name if they can possibly avoid it. "The man in whose house I live." "He whose rice I cook." "The father of my children"—anything that describes their husband, so long as they do not use his name. This, of course, applies only to the poorer or less educated Sinhalese and Tamils, and to those who cling to the old ideas of what constitutes the right attitude of women to the other sex.

The Buddhist religion is, theoretically, against caste, but that does not prevent its still existing amongst the Sinhalese, though they are gradually becoming less strict in its observance. The barbers, bootmakers, gipsies, and many others are of low caste, so are fishermen and hunters, because they take life, which is contrary to the teaching of Buddha. The Rodiyas too (their name is derived from a Sinhalese word meaning "filth") were long treated as outcasts—much as the "untouchables" in India—but gradually, under British rule, their condition has been altered and improved, and they now enjoy privileges formerly unknown by those poor creatures.

The wealthy Sinhalese are very kind to the poor

and aged, and the Buddhist priests, on going from door to door with their begging bowls, rarely meet with a rebuff, even the most humble folk finding something to give them. In the villages the people have most gracious manners. They are always courteous in addressing strangers, and willing to help them in any way they can. This, unfortunately, does not always apply to the Sinhalese of the towns, who are apt to adopt other and less pleasing ways. As a rule they are very superstitious, and that dread thing "the evil eye" is much feared, various charms being used to avert its evil influence on their cattle or other treasured possessions.

It is strange that with all Buddha's teaching about the sanctity of life, his followers in Ceylon never seem to have learnt how to be kind to animals. Although they will refrain from killing a snake because it is sacred, they will let their cattle or dogs go about with the most shocking sores, and never seem to show the slightest concern if they are ill. On the other hand they are very fond of their children, more especially if they are boys. Just at first, at all events, girls are apt to get a cold reception.

The Tamils who, except in the case of those who live in Jaffna, nearly all come over from Southern India to work on the estates, are quite different in temperament from the Sinhalese. Their manners are less attractive, their habits not always pleasing, but they have, in spite of those drawbacks, many good qualities, being industrious, good natured, and not without a sense of humour. In the intervals of work they discuss, in their limited vocabulary, their food or pay; take part in some weird, debased form of "saami" worship; or indulge in litigation, for which they have a perfect mania. They also like, whenever occasion offers, to pay visits to the nearest arrack tavern, where they become a little too merry at times.

Tamils have a great dislike to being made fun of in any way, and cannot bear to be laughed at. One day a young European Dorai, going the round of the workers, found the head cangany, who was in charge of a big gang of coolies, lying fast asleep under a tree. Instead of scolding him, his Master said in a loud, but quite pleasant voice, to one of the workers: "Ramsamy, I see poor Ramanathan is feeling a little tired this morning, please go to the bungalow and fetch a large easy chair for him; don't forget to bring some nice soft cushions as well." It was far more effective than any scolding; the cangany jumped to his feet, thoroughly ashamed, and furious with the coolies for the ripple of laughter with which they greeted their Master's sarcasm.

One of the principal Tamil festivals is "Thai Pongal" (or New Year's Day) which is held about the 14th of January. The newly harvested rice is then pounded and cooked with sugar, in new pots. If while it is cooking this mixture boils over, it is a sign that the year will be a lucky one, and that the crops will prosper, if not, only ill-luck is to be expected. After the rice has been eaten, the day is passed in various amusements, fireworks—the noisier the better—being specially popular.

Vale Festival, known on the estates as "Addi Poosay," is held in honour of a Hindu god, "Supramanion." Visits to the temple with offerings, calls on relations and friends, and general bustle and excitement go on for three days. There is also the festival of Dipawali, which is supposed to commemorate the release of the people from a certain wicked demon. It takes place in September, and for some reason it is considered necessary that those taking part in it should take a bath in oil, and also eat cakes made with oil. It would be quite useless to ask an ordinary Tamil for an explanation of this, or indeed of any of his customs. "Always doing that way," he will probably say with a grin—and leave it at that.

The Tamil weddings differ from those of the Sinhalese, and are more complicated affairs, especially amongst the rich Tamils of Jaffna. The bridegroom is expected to provide silk cloths (or sarongs) and turbans for the men guests, handsome cloths and jackets, as well as gold rings, for the women. A booth is erected in front of the house where the prospective bride lives. It must be sufficiently large to provide comfortable accommodation for all the guests, and is covered over, and all round, with cloth supplied by the family Dhoby. The entrance, as well as the inside, is elaborately decorated with large plantain leaves, evergreens, and flowers. A branch of a latex giving plant is placed on one side; it is taken from a tree supposed to be specially favoured by the gods, and is known as the "Arasanie." Its presence there is to induce the gods to enter the house, and give their blessing and approval of the marriage.

The bridegroom is met at some distance from the bride's home by her relations and friends, who have musicians to escort them. After much salaaming

DOUBLE BULLOCK CART

The bullock cart is more picturesque than comfortable, & a long journey in one is not to be recommended. The driver of this particular one has made it gay with coloured ornaments & tassels.

and good-natured chaff he is conducted to the booth but, rather ungraciously as it would seem, is not permitted to enter until he has given presents all round. When he has done this he is allowed to go in and seats himself, cross-legged, in front of a Brahman priest, who begins the wedding ceremony by repeating stanzas in Sanscrit, which, incidentally, nobody present is likely to understand in the least. Many curious rites are then gone through (about sixty in all): for example, the female cousins of the bridegroom light a small lamp with which they first touch his right, then his left knee and also his shoulders. The clothing he will wear later is blessed by the priest, then passed round to the relations—who also touch it by way of benison. Shortly after the bridegroom goes out, has a bath, shaves, and gives all his old clothes to the barber—then proceeds to worship at the nearest Hindu temple.

The bride, meanwhile, has been going through much the same performance (she, too, must retire to bathe), her old clothes afterwards being presented to the Dhoby. When the bridegroom returns from the temple his female cousins wash his feet with saffron water, and put gold or silver rings on his toes, then the bride and he sit down by the priest, who lights a fire (it must be made from the twigs of five latex giving trees) and makes the young couple swear by it, as well as by the "Arasanie," that they will be faithful. A tray containing nine different kinds of grain, and some milk having been brought, they again swear fidelity, the parents of both, as well as the priest, asking them if they will keep their promise. The "thalie," which takes the place of a wedding ring, is then tied round the neck of the bride. It is a band, or chain, of gold and is always worn by married Tamils. Water is poured over the hands of the couple by their parents, to show their responsibility towards them is over—they have washed their hands of the pair in fact—and the bride and bridegroom pour a little milk in each of the pots of grain. Later the grain will be planted, and its sprouting—or not—shows whether the married life will turn out a success, or the reverse.

Coco-nuts, and a grindstone, play an important part before the ceremony is over. They are placed near the relations who each take a nut, smash it on the grindstone, and approaching the newly married pair throw rice, grain of different kinds, and a special leaf, over their heads, repeating stanzas which express their good wishes. The couple in their turn break a coco-nut, and the bride placing her right foot on the grindstone, swears by it, and also by the sky to which her eyes are lifted, that she will ever be faithful and do her duty, after which the wedding, but for the feasting that follows, is over.

A BANYAN TREE

One of the banyan trees in Colombo which forms a remarkable natural arch in one of the residential streets.

CHAPTER XIII

MORE ABOUT THE PEOPLE

"Men are created one for another: either, then, teach them better, or bear with them."

BESIDES the Sinhalese, who now number about three millions, the Tamils born in Ceylon and those who have come over from India, there are a number of Burghers, Eurasians, Malays, Moors, the few Veddahs still left, as well as over eight thousand Europeans—mostly British—in the Island.

The Burghers form a very important part of the community; they are usually well educated, and fill many prominent Government and other posts. The term "Burgher" was originally applied only to descendants of the Dutch, but is now used rather indiscriminately, and frequently includes anyone who has a dash of European blood in his veins—Eurasians in fact.

The Malays are a quiet, industrious people who live peaceably with their neighbours, and keep to themselves a good deal. Moors are, for the most part, of Arab, South Indian, or Malay extraction, and are nearly all traders, more especially in gems. They live chiefly in Trincomalee and Galle, though they are to be found all over the Island. Those different peoples do not intermarry to any extent, nor do they mix with each other much, but they succeed in keeping on friendly terms as a rule.

The Ceylon University, several Colleges, and many schools where pupils are taught, either in English or in the vernacular, provide an excellent education. Missionaries have worked hard, not only to teach the Christian religion, but to help the poorer Natives in every possible way. Such modern movements as the Girl Guides, Boy Scouts, Child's Welfare Work —to mention only a few—are flourishing, but old ways and customs die hard in the East.

It is odd, when walking in Colombo along a street, full of handsome modern buildings, or shops displaying the latest European fashions, to turn round some corner on a party of devil dancers in their hideous masks, pirouetting about, and followed by tom-tom beaters in bizarre garments, on their way to some strange ceremony. A repulsive looking Native may pass, his forehead marked with sacred ashes, and his long black hair, matted and unclean, hanging over his shoulders. He has made some vow to his god, and until it has been fulfilled, must not cut or wash his straggling locks. In a little Hindu temple not far away some poor childless woman may be prostrating herself before one of the gods, as she implores the coveted gift of a son.

Even amongst the more educated Natives there are still not a few who would hesitate before saying a disrespectful word of Wahala Bandara Deviyo— who has the honour of being the chief demon in Ceylon. This dread deity (for he is really considered a god) lived originally on the top of a hill near Alutuwara, which is in the Kandyan district. When, however, the Gala Kepu Dewale (Hindu Temple) was built to his glory—or was it, perhaps, to conciliate him?—he condescended to move down and take up his abode there. He has stayed on, a perfect bogey! ever since.

This curious temple, which cannot, by any stretch of the imagination, be called beautiful, is visited every year by a number of pilgrims. They are mostly poor, half-demented women, who—or so they and their friends and relations believe—are suffering as a result of the evil influence of demons, and have come in the hope of getting relief. Probably many of them have tried all kinds of incantations before leaving their homes, but those having failed, they have thought it best to come straight to headquarters, and get the god himself to deal with the matter.

The principal room in the temple is divided into three compartments, which are separated from each other by curtains. In the middle one the demon is in residence, and just outside a priest is waiting to receive those possessed. He does this, dealing only with one case at a time, and being careful not to start operations until he has been presented with money, a few little objects, possibly made of silver, and betel. Those he puts away in a box, and then—in a loud, clear voice, begins to address the god.

"There is a woman here," he informs him, "who has a serious complaint to make. A demon has been molesting her, leading her a regular dance in fact, and she wishes it to be exorcised. Will the demon kindly attend to the matter at once, and order it to leave its victim in peace." Those may not actually be the words used, but they convey his meaning.

While the priest has been speaking, the woman has been moving about restlessly, shivering and shaking at intervals, and now and again uttering a loud cry, as if in terror. If there is no sign of her quieting down, the priest speaks more sharply to the god, announcing that if the demon is not turned out immediately he will proceed to take strong measures. Still the frightened woman fidgets and cries, and the priest then seizes a strong cane, lifts it threateningly and belabours her with it, striking her over and over again, until she suddenly—most likely the poor thing is exhausted—becomes perfectly still—the demon has fled! Her friends appear to offer congratulations, and lead her off in triumph, happy in the knowledge that she is cured. Strangely enough, when Natives have been known to be suffering from possession (or whatever the condition may be) for a long time, one visit to the demon god's temple is sufficient to keep them well for ever after, but perhaps it is not altogether surprising that they avoid the risk of another drastic thrashing.

Not far from the Gala Kepu Dewale are two rather interesting temples, those of Galadeniya and Lanatilake. The first is small, with a fine entrance porch. Inside there is a frieze of stone, with lions and tigers skilfully carved on it, which is worth looking at. There are also some curious carvings of females dancing and playing on musical instruments, that remind one just a little of those seen on friezes at Pompeii.

Lanatilake temple is a most picturesque building,

or rather group of buildings, with several gables, high-pitched roofs, and projecting eaves. The style of architecture is much favoured by the Kandyans, and is very effective. The temple is perched high up on a rock, and at the first glance is not unlike a Christian church. Cave, in his interesting book on Ceylon, mentions writers who have compared it to some of the old churches in Norway.

Inside it is so dark and gloomy that it is difficult to see the crude pictures with which the walls and ceilings are elaborately decorated. In the main building there is a gigantic figure of Buddha; he is seated under a canopy which is held over him by weird-looking female figures. On the doorways and arches are uncanny mythical animals, that stare stonily with ugly protruding eyes, and there are several garish deities covered in tinsel and sham jewels. As in all Hindu temples, the odour of flowers that are piled in front of the various gods, makes it so oppressive that it is impossible to stay long enough to examine the different objects very carefully.

When motoring one occasionally notices small buildings, in which parties of dark-skinned folks may be resting. They are Natives on some journey, and usually they have several half-clad children clinging to them, passing the time in sucking sugar cane, or munching half-ripe bananas, while their elders chew betel. The buildings are of a square shape as a rule, open all round, and with a high roof, supported on pillars which are sometimes carved with the sacred cobras and geese, or other animals. Those " Ambalams " as they are called, are generally provided by some rich and charitably disposed person. They are a real boon to the poorer Natives during the hottest part of the day, or in the heavy rains of the monsoon.

In the more remote parts of the Island where the motor has not yet penetrated, romance still lingers. One Wesak—or Buddha's birthday—two Europeans went to a small village in the Bintenne district, to spend a few days. They had to ride many miles, a good part of their way being by a road that passed through the jungle. Once or twice they had an experience that was alarming for the moment, but turned out to be quite harmless. To ride through a herd of semi-wild buffaloes, for example, was not exactly pleasant, but the ungainly animals kept their noses in the air, in the supercilious way buffaloes always do, and went on. A big elephant suddenly emerged from the jungle, and for a second or two the riders felt their hearts beat uncomfortably, as the possibility of its being a "rogue" flashed across them. The appearance of its Mahout was reassuring and they rode on, laughing at their needless fear. Now and again, too, the ponies shuddered, or stopped dead, as a snake glided across their path, but in each case it was of an innoxious kind, and soon disappeared.

It was getting dusk as the travellers approached the little Rest House. As they left the jungle behind and crossed a stretch of wide park-like country, they came upon a large company of Sinhalese, camping under the tamarind and other trees that were dotted here and there. These Natives had lit small fires which flared in the dim light, and were cooking their simple meal of rice, which is still their principal food. It is eaten with sugar or *ghee* (clarified butter), sometimes quite plain—except for having a few chillies added; and the water in which it is cooked (known as cungee) is also used very often as a simple beverage. Apparently they were all as happy as children, judging by the laughter and chattering that were going on It came as a surprise when they saw two weary riders, followed by their horsekeepers, and a string of coolies laden with baggage and provisions; for a moment they seemed doubtful about the intruders, but a few good-natured remarks, in their own language, put them at their ease, and a crowd of them gathered round, eager to see their unexpected visitors.

" Lady " was evidently of special interest, and a woman volunteered the information that she, and one or two of the others, had never seen a white woman before—they came from a village in the jungle. That accounted for the excitement of some of those who came uncomfortably close, touching " Lady's " riding habit with curious fingers, pointing to her gloves—which seemed specially to amuse them—and staring at her, not rudely, but with a sort of surprised interest. After a time, when it had been explained that the visitors had ridden many miles and were tired, the Natives salaamed and wandered back to their cooking, discussing the new arrivals with embarrassing frankness, probably not quite realizing that one of them understood every word they said.

Next morning it was delightful to wake up in that quiet spot, and to see the first rays of light filtering through the tall palms and clumps of giant bamboos. The blossoms of some " coral " trees were just beginning to show their vivid scarlet, birds were twittering and calling to each other on the branches, and there was a tinkling of bells, as a string of *tavalams* (small bullocks used for carrying loads) moved slowly along, their drivers looking shadowy and ghostlike in the dim light. Several Sinhalese went by to their work in the paddy fields, and a few naked children climbed and sprawled on the verandah, eager to see as much of the strangers as they possibly could.

A little later a rather pompous Eurasian, in an oddly cut suit of immaculately clean white linen, and a painfully high, stiff collar, came to pay his respects. He announced, talking very slowly, that he was the Dispenser of the district, adding with more frankness than modesty, that he had passed "many severe examinations in a first-class way," and was "a very learned fellow." He stayed a long time and his flowery speeches were a little trying, but he meant well, and before leaving, presented a basketful of fruit, which was very welcome.

He had only just gone when an old Sinhalese man appeared; he must have been nearly eighty, but looked about a hundred, so wrinkled and wizened was his rather fine old face. He was staggering under the weight of a huge bunch of bananas, which he offered, after making a profound salaam and informing "Lady" and "Master" that they were his Mother and Father—a statement that might have been a trifle startling, had they not understood an Eastern compliment.

Two pretty Native girls were the next visitors. They had been loitering near the verandah for some time, before screwing up sufficient courage to present a stiff little bouquet of flowers and a few mangoes. They were dreadfully shy, keeping their eyes down, and rubbing their bare feet nervously one against the other, as the two Europeans spoke to them; also they had not the least idea when to bring their visit to an end, and had to be given a rather broad hint before they thought it necessary to go.

Out by the temple the scene was a busy one. Worshippers, in their best garments of many colours—it was Buddha's birthday and they were honouring it in every way they could—were coming and going constantly, each carrying an offering of flowers. The dagoba near, which is of great age, and enshrines a lock of Buddha's *blue* hair, was showing signs of falling to pieces, and was being repaired. That was the reason why two Buddhist priests were standing at its base by a pile of bricks. Those were handed out to the people, as many as they could conveniently carry, and they gave in exchange as much money as they could—it was not much—to buy a fresh supply. They carried the bricks on their heads as they made the by no means easy ascent to the top of the dagoba, pleased to feel they were helping to repair it, and were acquiring merit at the same time.

The priests, their faces half hidden as usual by their palm-leaf fans, glanced surreptitiously from time to time at the Europeans, puzzled as to why they were there and watching the whole proceedings with such interest. They seemed much astonished when one of the strangers asked, in Sinhalese, whether he and "Lady" might also carry up some bricks to help restore the dagoba, at the same time offering a few rupees. More accustomed to cents than rupees, the priests' faces brightened considerably, though they looked incredulous. Did "Lady" and "Master" really think they could carry bricks? They did—always provided they were not expected to carry them on their heads, on the top of their sun hats—so they were provided with one or two, to the intense delight of all the Natives round, who laughed to see the clumsy efforts of the strangers to clamber over the loose stones with their unaccustomed burden. But they were pleased, those simple folks, and though the climb was a bit tiring and difficult, it was worth a greater effort for the sake of the view at the top. In any case the visitors were more than repaid by the pleasure their taking part had so obviously given.

A little later they were rowed across the river in a raft, made of planks roughly tied together. Over the lilies and reeds with which the edge of the water was fringed, brilliant blue moths and butterflies of every colour were hovering, and the chorus of birds was only marred, now and again, by the rasping sound of the "scissors grinders" (cicadas) or the hoarse croaking of frogs.

"Master" went off shooting while "Lady" sat down under a shady tamarind tree with a book. She was alone, with the exception of her horse-keeper who had been left on guard, but in a very short time she was surrounded by Natives, who seemed to suddenly spring from nowhere. They squatted round, all chattering at once, and evidently discussing her freely. As her book happened to be illustrated, she showed them the pictures, at which they looked with interest, even when holding them upside down. But their attentions were a little trying and "Master" was hailed with delight on his return.

It was pleasant to get back to the cool Rest House shortly after, for the heat had become intense, and to find a tiffin of curry, snipe, and delicious fruit ready. The table decoration consisted of pink and yellow paper twisted into a fantastic design with dusty bottles into which some red hibiscus flowers and purple bougainvillea had been tightly packed, but the visitors (may they be forgiven!) assured the smiling Rest House keeper that he had arranged everything beautifully.

Time went very quickly in that peaceful spot; it was a real pleasure to get to know a little more of those friendly people and their ways. But "the best of things beyond their measure cloy," so it was perhaps just as well that it was not possible to remain until the glamour had worn off, but soon became necessary to return to a rather more conventional life.

CHAPTER XIV

CONCLUSION

OVID mentions Ceylon, or "Taprobane" as it was known in his day, as being exceedingly remote, and indeed it was, until modern steamships changed conditions, and brought the lovely Island within comparatively easy reach of Europe. The voyage is a pleasant one, even the intense heat to be felt at times when passing through the Red Sea, need no longer be dreaded, owing to the general use of electric fans on the big liners. It is, however, as well for those who are indifferent sailors to avoid the monsoons whenever possible—October till May being considered the best months during which to travel East.

Although railways in Ceylon are well managed, and good accommodation is always provided for travellers, there is no doubt that the ideal way in which to get about the Island is by motor. Unfortunately motoring comes rather expensive, particularly if cars have to be hired, as the charge made invariably includes the return journey. There are public motor buses in some places, but—as has already been mentioned, they are rarely used by Europeans, and leave much to be desired. Some day they will be improved, though it is certainly true that the East cannot be hustled, and it will take time.

Aviation

As coolies nearly always carry baggage on their heads, the merciful traveller avoids too large or heavy boxes, and it is almost unnecessary to say that, in addition to the fixed tariff of charges, a *santossum* (tip) is always expected, and if not produced, will be unblushingly demanded. It is wise to err on the side of generosity, for coolies, more especially in the towns, can be very fluent on occasions. Their language may not be understood, but there is never any doubt as to the nature of their remarks, which are uncomplimentary to say the least of it.

So far aviation as a means of getting about has not become popular in Ceylon. It seems rather doubtful if it ever will, as the ranges of hills and the steamy heat in the low country, make it difficult to fly long distances. Some of the naval aircraft pilots, when they happen to be in Colombo, take the opportunity of flying about the coast and district, to the delight of the Natives, who are much impressed. Otherwise aeroplanes are seldom to be seen.

From modern flying machines to primitive Sinhalese catamarans is a far cry, but some pleasant hours may be spent in one of these canoes, which are more comfortable than they look, and have the merit of being very safe. It is possible to go out in a catamaran at Batticalo, for instance, a peaceful little place on the East Coast, and, at the same time, to have a chance of hearing the so-called "singing fish" which are a peculiarity of that part of the Island.

After dinner, on a moonlight night, it is delightful to skim across the dark waters of the lagoon, and listen for the faint musical sounds, like the tinkling of fairy bells, that sometimes come, so mysteriously, from the depths below. What causes them ? Are they the far distant strains of music made by some lover serenading his mermaid mistress, as she combs her long tresses in a cave away down amongst the corals ? Or is the Sinhalese boatman right when he declares—with a contemptuous sniff : "that only ye' sounds coming from ye' shells" (Sinhalese always preface the letter "S" by "ye" for some odd reason). He never heard of mermaids, and obviously scorns the idea of singing fish. But what does it matter ?—nothing seems to matter to those who feel the enchantment of an Eastern night.

How quiet it is out there on the lagoon. There is only the gentle splash of the water as it kisses the shore, now and again the melancholy moan of an owl, or cry of some night bird. The Natives are out fishing, a few of them moving about, with torches that flicker here and there, like will-o'-the-wisps dancing by the sea, and stars shine brilliantly in a cloudless canopy of blue ; the palms looking like sleepy giants as they nod under the touch of a light breeze.

In the early morning the water looks so inviting that it makes one impatient to get into its coolness. If visitors have forgotten suitable garments, they may be glad to know that pyjamas and sun topees will meet the situation They have been worn at Batticalo by those bathing, and nobody has shown the least surprise—but that is another story. Sun topees, by the way, must not be forgotten, for the sun blazes down fiercely at times, and a headache is the least of the evils it may produce.

Snakes

After a swim it is a joy to rest under the shady trees, and watch the fishing boats cruising along the coast, while a Sinhalese *podian* climbs the nearest coco-nut palm, to bring down nuts filled with grateful liquid. Before getting comfortably settled, however, it is wise to look about carefully, in case some snake may be wriggling unpleasantly near.

Snakes are always a possible danger, though there are, fortunately, not a great many tic polongas and cobras (the most dangerous of the reptiles to be found in Ceylon) at all events in the more frequented parts of the Island. There are timid visitors who seem to imagine snakes are to be met everywhere—even in the streets of the towns. One nervous lady, waking on her first night at the G. O. H. caught sight of a pink ribbon (meant for tying up the mosquito curtains when these were not in use); it was dangling suspiciously over her bed, and she sat up shrieking, "A snake—oh! a snake," until an indignant Ayah appeared, to inform her scornfully: "Snakes not made of ribbons in this country, Missy." All the same it does not do to forget that there *are* such creatures, or to omit reasonable care in avoiding them.

In some ways, Batticalo is quite up-to-date, and, amongst its inhabitants, it includes at least one literary aspirant. Once, when a small party of Europeans were spending a few days there, they were lazing in the verandah (feeling at peace with all the world, after a tiffin consisting of seer fish, dressed crab, prawn curry, and jaggery pudding), when a rather smudgy visiting card was brought to them by the Appu (head servant) on which was inscribed in bold letters "Joseph Daniel David."

"That," he hesitated, "Dorai on ye' steps, I telling him better not coming in." The Appu spoke in a rather disapproving tone. It is curious what snobs all Native servants are; they quickly classify people, and it is by no means a question of clothing, or even tips. If they decide a man is not a "real" Dorai their manner to him will be perfectly polite, but notably colder. Evidently the Appu had doubts about this visitor; the name on the card was intriguing, however, and he was told to show in its owner.

Mr. Joseph Daniel David was a tall, thin Eurasian who wore peculiar garments. His flaming red tie might have meant that he favoured Communism, his long black coat that his profession was that of a cleric of sorts, while his wide, baggy, grey trousers suggested he had been, during one period of his career, at Oxford. With a flourish he removed a spotlessly white topee—an unnecessary addition to his toilet, considering how long and thick were his oily black locks—and made an elaborate bow.

"May I be pardoned this apparently seeming untimely intrusion," he began, in the mincing tone of voice his kind usually adopt, "but having been informed, in a roundabout fashion, that present company were here, I decided to make the bold attempt to call. Have I the honour to address——?" He bowed again to one of the company, who admitted being the person named.

"As I have decided to embark on a literary career and to write books also," continued Mr. Joseph

Daniel David, "I have the express hope of enlisting esteemed advice, and valuable assistance."

The Europeans tried to look intelligent, but tiffin had made them sleepy, and they realized their visitor's call might be a lengthy one.

"Yes," murmured one of them, politely stifling a yawn, "and in what way?"

"My case may be briefly stated in this fashion, Lady." He began a long, rambling explanation which was difficult to follow, because he used words which must have been extracted from a dictionary for the occasion, and more for their length than lucidity. It was, however, gathered by the end of his speech that his chief ambition in life was to write. He had consulted a young English engineer who had advised him to form his style on that of Miss Ethel Dell—"one first-class writer" as he said—only it had occurred to him that, before finally deciding which particular style to adopt, it might be well to give other authors a chance. He had recently heard there was a gentleman called Mr. Bernard Shaw, was he perhaps considered in England to be as good a writer as Miss Ethel Dell?

The two names in conjunction were unexpected—one of the party hastily enveloped himself in a newspaper, which shook suspiciously. The visitor glanced at it: "I am come only to solicit kind information," he said with some dignity.

"Of course, and we shall be delighted to help. If you will come into the next room, I'll write a list of our best-known writers for you."

With a reproachful look at the newspaper, one of the party rose and led the way, followed by Mr.

Joseph Daniel David, after he had made another low bow.

He waited patiently while the list, a rather long one, was made out, and then looked at it critically: "You have plenty writers in England, men and women also," he remarked. "This Mr. Shakespeare now, he lived a long time ago. I think he is a little too old fashioned, h'm? And Mr. Robert Louis Stevenson also, but my friend Pereira says he was a poet. I also am a poet, perhaps you might say, a minor one," he added modestly.

"That is very interesting—what sort of poetry do you write? Won't you repeat some of it to me?"

"My latest effort is a poor thing—a mere trifle, yet I will say it." He struck an attitude, and began:

> "Oh! come to my arms oh! come,
> I've loved you since last Aut-*umn*,
> And straight from my heart's bot-*tom*,
> Oh! come to my arms then—Come."

"Thank you so much. It's—it's most original," stammered the listener in a shaky voice. "Is that all? It's so—so short."

"Yes, Lady, but I can of course make longer poems. I wish to keep my best efforts for my book, however. When it appears I will send you a copy—with poems complete."

So far his *magnum opus* has never appeared, but if some day a wonderful book is printed, bearing the name Joseph Daniel David, it is well to know that the author may be found at Batticalo.

Dug-outs

After having been out in a catamaran, visitors may feel inclined to try the quaint looking boats Natives use on the river at Kaltura. They are made of two dug-outs, connected by a platform, on which there is a shelter constructed with plaited fronds of coco-nut palms. The little boats go along very slowly, but for those who care for beautiful scenery —and that on the river between Kaltura and Ratnapura is exquisite—the leisurely pace will be rather an advantage than otherwise.

Kaltura is an attractive town, with many charming old Dutch houses, some of them in gardens full of all kinds of gay flowers, creepers, and shrubs. The Natives there have a special industry in baskets, and the women and children may be seen, seated under the huge Banyan trees or palms, busy weaving. The baskets are made in all kinds of shapes but the most popular are those arranged in nests of twelve, which fit in to each other, and are easily packed. They are made of fronds of palm which are split into narrow slips, dyed black, red, and yellow, and then woven.

At Ratnapura, a little town surrounded by ranges of hills, the gem digger may be seen at work. It is always exciting to watch operations, for, although unfortunately a good many of the precious stones have flaws, one of great value may appear at any moment. The colours, more especially of the blue sapphires, are very fine. Moonstones are so common that they are not much valued, but they are exceedingly pretty stones when set in either silver or gold. The Sinhalese have a special admiration for the "Ca''s eye," chiefly because it is rare, but it lacks colour, and is rather cold. Europeans used at one time to amuse themselves hunting for gems; the trade, however, is now entirely in the hands of Natives.

Many interesting and helpful books have been written about Ceylon. A comparatively recent one is by Major A. M. Enriquez. It is called *Ceylon: Past and Present.* All the works of H. Cave are most useful to those interested in the Island. Tennent, Valentyn, and Percival's books are excellent, while the story of his life and adventures by Robert Knox is a book—as has already been mentioned—of great charm. The *Mahawansa* (Chronicles of the Great) has been translated, and will delight those who like picturesque Oriental imagery, and highly coloured, wildly improbable, but fascinating tales of the East. It is supposed to be the most authentic of all the Sinhalese chronicles.

But books, however well written, never convey the subtle charm of the "Island of Jewels"—it has to be seen to be appreciated. There almost seems to be three Ceylons now—that which consists of towns with modern buildings, palatial hotels equipped with jazz bands, wireless, not always a success it is said, owing to the difficulty with atmospherics—and other up-to-date attractions (?); another in which are to be found well-ordered tea, rubber, and kindred estates, with trim bungalows and factories, in which are all the latest inventions in the way of machinery, etc., and the last—the real Ceylon, the land "where every prospect pleases," full of wild beauty, history, and romance.

This is the Ceylon that lingers in the memory when the day comes to sail away to colder climes. Those who have the time and opportunity to travel have a great pleasure in store if they arrange to visit the Island, for the charm of it will be an abiding memory. On grey days, when the rain falls, the wind blows, and it is cold and cheerless, they will remember the sunshine of the East, the fascination of the scenery, the kindly Sinhalese people, and the fragrance of the flowers. "God gave us memory that we might have roses in December."

Index

Index

Index

Index